P9-BUI-661

---

# THE MISSILE CRISIS

---

---

# THE MISSILE CRISIS

## BY ELIE ABEL

BANTAM BOOKS · TORONTO · NEW YORK · LONDON

THE MISSILE CRISIS

*A Bantam Book / published by arrangement with
J. B. Lippincott Company*

PRINTING HISTORY

*J. B. Lippincott Company edition published February 1966
2nd printing .... February 1966
Bantam edition published September 1966*

*Bantam Books are published by Bantam Books, Inc., a subsidiary
of Grosset & Dunlap, Inc. Its trade-mark, consisting of the words
"Bantam Books" and the portrayal of a bantam, is registered in the
United States Patent Office and in other countries. Marca Registrada.
Bantam Books, Inc., 271 Madison Avenue, New York, N.Y. 10016.*

PRINTED IN THE UNITED STATES OF AMERICA

FOR MY PARENTS

# ACKNOWLEDGEMENTS

This narrative owes much to the recollections of some three dozen men who, in greater or lesser degree, were engaged in or privy to the missile crisis deliberations. I am particularly indebted to:

Dean Acheson, former Secretary of State; Admiral George W. Anderson Jr., former Chief of Naval Operations; William Attwood, American Ambassador to Kenya; George W. Ball, Under-Secretary of State; Charles E. Bohlen, American Ambassador to France; William H. Brubeck, political counsellor, American Embassy London; David K. E. Bruce, American Ambassador to the Court of St James's; McGeorge Bundy, special assistant to the President of the United States; Abram J. Chayes, former legal adviser, Department of State; Douglas Dillon, former Secretary of the Treasury; Clayton Fritchey, information counsellor, US Mission to the United Nations; Roswell Gilpatric, former Deputy Secretary of Defense; James L. Greenfield, Assistant Secretary of State; Lord Harlech, former British Ambassador to the United States; Roger Hilsman, former director of Intelligence and Research, Department of State; Thomas L. Hughes Jr, Director of Intelligence and Research, Department of State; Philip M. Kaiser, American Minister in London; Senator Robert F. Kennedy; Robert Manning, former Assistant Secretary of State; John McCone, former Director of the Central Intelligence Agency; Robert S. McNamara, Secretary of Defense; Paul M. Nitze, Secretary of the Navy; Kenneth P. O'Donnell, former special assistant to the President; Dean Rusk, Secretary of State; Pierre Salinger, former press secretary to the President; John Scali, American Broadcasting Company; Frank A. Sieverts, special assistant, bureau of public affairs, Department of State; Theodore C. Sorensen, former special counsel to President Kennedy; the late Adlai E. Stevenson; Major General Sir Kenneth William Dobson Strong, Director of the Joint Intelligence Bureau, British Ministry of Defence; Arthur Sylvester, Assistant Secretary of Defense; Llewellyn E. Thompson, Ambassador at Large; Donald M. Wilson, former deputy director, United States Information Agency.

A good many others helped in piecing out the narrative, some by providing documentary material never before published. Special acknowledgement is due to my wife, Corinne Prevost Abel, and to my secretary, Sara Evans.

London                                                    ELIE ABEL

# CONTENTS

SUNDAY, *October 14, 1962*     1
MONDAY, *October 15*     17
TUESDAY, *October 16*     31
WEDNESDAY, *October 17*     43
THURSDAY, *October 18*     54
FRIDAY, *October 19*     69
SATURDAY, *October 20*     76
SUNDAY, *October 21*     84
MONDAY, *October 22*     95
TUESDAY, *October 23*     110
WEDNESDAY, *October 24*     123
THURSDAY, *October 25*     139
FRIDAY, *October 26*     152
SATURDAY, *October 27*     165
SUNDAY, *October 28*     180
*Postscript*     187
*Index*     194

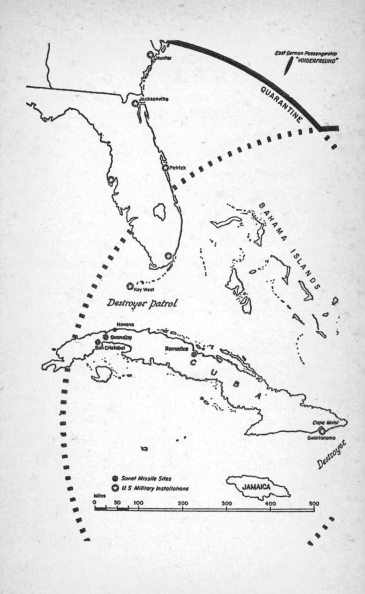

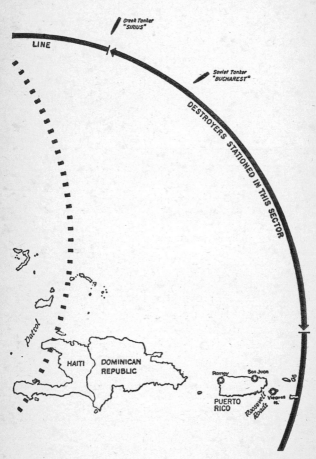

# SUNDAY
## OCTOBER 14, 1962

*I know there is no present evidence, and I think there is no present likelihood that the Cubans and the Cuban Government and the Soviet Government would, in combination, attempt to install a major offensive capability.*
—MCGEORGE BUNDY in a television interview, October 14, 1962

IT was the kind of Sunday that involves millions of Americans in the change of seasons: blue haze over the suburbs and the smell of burning leaves in the air; country roads crowded with the automobiles of city people come to see the green summer woods splashed with the flaming reds, russets, and yellows of autumn; the time of year when football coaches pass for the wisest of men, to judge by the columns of type allotted to their prophecies in the swollen Sunday newspapers. As this happened to be an even-numbered year the wise men of the gridiron were obliged to share space with the politicians, at least until the first Tuesday in November, Election Day. And among politicians, the outs talked chiefly of Cuba that October, holding the ins to blame for tolerating a Communist dictatorship 90 miles off the Florida coast. Just as the outs two years before had blamed the ins for allowing that dictatorship to establish itself in power.

Now the outs of 1960 had become the ins of 1962, roles reversed even if the rhetoric was substantially unchanged. Two years before, the leader of the outs, Senator John Fitzgerald Kennedy of Massachusetts, had been the attacker. In a campaign speech at Johns-

1

town, Pennsylvania, on October 15, 1960, Kennedy had said of his Republican rival, Richard Milhous Nixon: "Mr. Nixon hasn't mentioned Cuba very prominently in this campaign. He talks about standing firm in Berlin, standing firm in the Far East, standing up to Khrushchev. But he never mentions standing firm in Cuba. And if you can't stand up to Castro, how can you be expected to stand up to Khrushchev. . . . The transformation of Cuba into a Communist base of operations a few minutes from our coast—by jet plane, missile or submarine—is an incredibly dangerous development to have been permitted by our Republican policy-makers."

This time it was Republicans who attacked Democrats for doing nothing to get rid of Fidel Castro's regime. This time it was *President* John Fitzgerald Kennedy on the defensive, ridiculing Senator Homer E. Capehart, the Indiana Republican, who had advocated an immediate invasion of Cuba. The newspapers that Sunday morning had Kennedy saying in a Saturday campaign speech at Indianapolis: "Those self-appointed generals and admirals who want to send someone else's sons to war . . . ought to be kept at home by the voters and replaced by someone who has some understanding of what the 20th Century is all about."

Congress had adjourned Saturday afternoon its longest session since the Korean War, one of the bitterest ever. In the dying hours of that session, Senator Kenneth Keating, the New York Republican, sounded the alarm. He said his own sources of information "which have been 100 per cent reliable" had substantiated a report that six intermediate-range missile sites were under construction in Cuba. Keating called on the Kennedy Administration to confirm or deny these reports. The date was October 10. Keating did not specify the location. Nor would he divulge his sources when pressed, both officially and privately, by his friend John A. McCone, Director of the Central Intelligence Agency. McCone was himself a Republican.

He had long suspected that the Russians might be tempted to put ballistic missiles into Cuba, though he lacked the proof Keating now claimed to possess.

At three o'clock on that Sunday in October, Mc-George Bundy, the Harvard dean turned Presidential assistant for national security affairs, sat in the Washington studios of the American Broadcasting Company, being interviewed on television by Edward P. Morgan and John Scali. Without naming Keating, Morgan inquired about the Administration's consistent denials that the Soviet military installations in Cuba were offensive in nature.

MORGAN: Isn't it possible, isn't it really possible, that these could be converted into offensive weapons virtually overnight and if so what would we do?

BUNDY: Well, I don't myself think that there is any present—I know there is no present evidence, and I think there is no present likelihood that the Cubans and the Cuban Government and the Soviet Government would, in combination, attempt to install a major offensive capability.

Now, it is true that these words "offensive" and "defensive," if you try to apply them precisely to every single item, mislead you. Whether a gun is offensive or defensive depends a little bit on which end you are on. It is also true that the MIG fighters which have been put into Cuba for more than a year now, and any possible additions in the form of aircraft, might have a certain marginal capability for moving against the United States. But I think we have to bear in mind the relative magnitudes here. The United States is not going to be placed in any position of major danger to its own security in Cuba, and we are not going to permit that situation to develop. That, I think, is what the Administration had been trying to make clear. So far, everything that has been delivered in Cuba falls within the categories of aid which the Soviet Union has provided, for example, to neutral states like Egypt or Indonesia, and I should not be surprised to see additional military assistance of that sort. That is not going to turn an island of six million people, with five or six thousand technicians and specialists, into a major threat to the United States, and I believe most of the American people do not share the views of the few who have acted as if suddenly this kind of military support created a mortal threat to us. It does not.

Bundy was dismissing as simply beyond belief Mc-Cone's notion that the Soviet Union might be tempted by Cuba's proximity to the United States, sufficiently tempted to turn the island into a strategic base. It was a notion, as Bundy had special reason to know, already seriously examined within the closed society of American intelligence chiefs. John McCone had been the first to turn the possibility over in his mind. He possessed no proof, nor even persuasive evidence. But McCone could not rid himself of that nagging suspicion. Nor was McCone the only Washington official nagged by suspicion. The October 1 issue of *Aviation Week and Space Technology* reported: "Pentagon strategists consider the present arms build-up in Cuba the first step toward eventual construction of intermediate-range ballistic missile emplacements. They point out that the defensive nature of armaments arriving from Soviet Russia is aimed at preventing aerial photographic reconnaissance, not at preparations to fend off invasion. . . ." Nikita Khrushchev, Chairman of the Soviet Council of Ministers and First Secretary of the Communist Party, had more than once boasted that he needed no missile bases in Cuba to protect the island against aggression from the United States; Soviet missiles were sufficiently accurate and powerful to reach targets in the United States from Russian soil. As far back as July 10, 1960, when John Kennedy was still the junior Senator from Massachusetts, Khrushchev had said:

Figuratively speaking, if need be, Soviet artillery-men can support the Cuban people with their rocket fire if aggressive forces in the Pentagon dare to start intervention against Cuba.

Again, on January 2, 1961, seventeen days before John Kennedy's inauguration as President, Khrushchev denounced the idea that Russia was contemplating missile bases in Cuba. At a Cuban Embassy reception in Moscow, Khrushchev said:

Alarming news is coming from Cuba at present, news that the most aggressive American monopolists are preparing a direct attack on Cuba. What is more, they are trying to present the case as though rocket bases of the Soviet Union are being set up or are already established in Cuba. It is well known that this is a foul slander. There are no Soviet military bases in Cuba; in the same way there are no such bases in other countries.

In April of 1961, following the disastrous attempt to land a brigade of American-trained Cuban exiles at Bahía de Cochinos (The Bay of Pigs), Khrushchev sent President Kennedy two notes. The first was a warning that Cuba could count on Soviet support "in beating back" any armed attack. The second again sought to reassure the United States that the Soviet leadership would keep its missiles at home. Khrushchev wrote:

As for the Soviet Union we have stated on many occasions and I am stating again that our government does not seek any advantages or privileges in Cuba. We do not have any bases in Cuba, and we do not intend to establish any.

Thus the record was clear. The coterie of Washington specialists on Soviet affairs saw no reason to challenge Khrushchev's public statements. The Russians had never stationed medium- or long-range missiles on the territories of other nations, not even on the terri-

tories of their Warsaw Pact allies. It seemed highly
improbable that they would do in Cuba what they had
never done in Poland or Hungary.

In July of 1962, Fidel Castro sent his brother, Raul,
Cuba's Defense Minister, on an unexplained visit to
Moscow. Then, beginning in late July, United States
Navy reconnaissance planes observed a stream of ships
making for Cuba out of Soviet ports on the Baltic and
Black Seas. The sudden increase in tonnage wakened
the curiosity of American intelligence agencies. Much
of this new traffic docked at Mariel, a deep-water port
on the northern coast of Pinar del Río province. From
agents in Cuba, the CIA soon heard that Mariel had
been transformed. Cubans living near the docks had
been forced to evacuate their homes and Russian sentries guarded the docks while other Russians unloaded the waiting ships.

On August 24, a full week before Senator Keating
delivered the first of his ten speeches warning of a Soviet military build-up in Cuba, the State Department
invited reporters to a background briefing by Roger
Hilsman, director of its Intelligence and Research office. Hilsman's information, attributed under the rules
governing conferences of this kind to "United States
officials" or "official sources," amounted to this: between July 26 and August 8, eight Soviet-bloc ships
had arrived in Cuba. Perhaps a dozen more had
docked between August 9 and 24. They carried large
quantities of transportation, electronic and construction equipment—communications and radar vans,
trucks, mobile generators.

"From what we have observed of this cargo," Hilsman speculated, "it appears that much of it will go into
the improvement of coastal and air defenses. It may
include surface-to-air missiles, which the Soviets have
already supplied to Iraq and Indonesia."

He also reported the arrival of some 3,000 to 5,000
Soviet military technicians, noted that they did not appear to be organized in combat units, and that they

were never seen in uniform, mostly in slacks and sports shirts. It was Hilsman's assumption that the Russians were there to install an antiaircraft missile system and to teach the Cubans how to operate it. Within five days United States intelligence knew for certain that some of the crates unloaded in Mariel and other Cuban ports contained surface-to-air (SAM) missiles. On August 29, a U-2 plane flying over western Cuba captured the first photographic proof of two SAMs in position. Six more were tentatively located.

Two days before Hilsman's briefing, McCone had met privately with President Kennedy. The intelligence chief, a widower, was leaving Washington the following day to marry Theiline McGee Pigott, a Seattle widow. His own recollection is that he told Kennedy: "The only construction I can put on the material going into Cuba is that the Russians are preparing to introduce offensive missiles. I question the value of SAMs except as a means of making possible the introduction of offensive missiles." McCone also confided his suspicions to the Secretary of the Treasury, Douglas Dillon, at a dinner party on the eve of his departure for the wedding trip to Cap Ferrat, on the French Riviera.

McCone, admittedly, was speculating. Ever since the spring of 1962—before there was any evidence of SAMs going into Cuba—he had suspected that the Russians might install offensive missiles. His reasoning was based on simple geography: for the first time the Russians had access to "a piece of real estate" within easy reach of the United States. Missiles of roughly 1,000-mile range installed in Cuba could not reach back to the Soviet Union if they should ever be turned around. McCone believed that the reason the Russians had not installed similar missiles in the satellite countries was that they did not trust Poles or Hungarians with nuclear weapons capable of leveling Moscow if they could be turned to the east. Within the intelligence community, some professionals smiled indulgently at McCone's seemingly fantastic conception. The first intimation of SAMs arriving in Cuba hardened his suspicion. He asked himself whether the Russians could be so naive as to believe that anti-aircraft missiles, by themselves, would guarantee Cuba against a serious invasion attempt from the United States. And having rejected the thought, he determined to his own satisfaction that the SAMs were being installed to protect something else—possibly offensive missiles trained on the United States.

Not until September 2 did the Russians say a public word about their arms build-up in Cuba. In a communiqué issued that day, concerning a second Cuban visit to Moscow by Ernesto (Che) Guevara, Castro's Minister of Industries, and his militia chief, Emilio Aragones Navarro, the Kremlin announced that the Cuban Government (at an unspecified date) had requested help in the form of "armaments" and "specialists for training Cuban servicemen." The Soviet Government said it had agreed to supply both, in view of certain threats from "aggressive imperialist quarters with regard to Cuba." The communiqué added: "As long as the above-mentioned quarters continue to threaten Cuba, the Cuban Republic has every justification for taking necessary measures to insure its sovereignty and independence, while all Cuba's true friends have every right to respond to this legitimate request."

Lest President Kennedy become unduly alarmed over the extent of the arms build-up, Nikita Khrushchev, on September 4, sent the Soviet Ambassador in Washington, Anatoliy Dobrynin, to call on the President's brother, Attorney General Robert Kennedy. Dobrynin said he had a message from Khrushchev for the President, to be communicated only through his brother. It boiled down to a promise that the Soviet Union would create no trouble for the United States—in Berlin or Southeast Asia—during the election campaign.

Robert Kennedy, aware of CIA reports that eight SAM sites were already established in Cuba, replied that Khrushchev had stirred up trouble enough by sending arms to Fidel Castro. Dobrynin was warmly reassuring. He was not aware the Soviet Union had sent missiles of any kind to Cuba, Dobrynin said, stressing that his government certainly did not propose to place in the hands of any third party the power to involve the Soviet Union in a thermonuclear war.

Later that day, Robert Kennedy gave the President a detailed account of his conversation with Dobrynin. Far from being mollified by the Soviet Ambassador's words, he urged the President to warn the Russians in unmistakable terms that American tolerance of Soviet missilery in Cuba had its limits. The Attorney General and his deputy, Nicholas de B. Katzenbach, helped to draft the warning issued the same day in President Kennedy's name. It said that the introduction of offensive ground-to-ground missiles into Cuba, or of "other significant offensive capability" either in Cuban hands or under Russian direction, would raise issues of the gravest kind. The President pledged himself to prevent, by whatever means might be necessary, armed action by the Castro regime against any part of the Western Hemisphere. On September 7, Kennedy requested Congressional authorization to call up 150,-000 reserve troops. Congress agreed.

Once again, on September 11, Moscow disclaimed any hostile intent. "There is no need," the Kremlin said, "for the Soviet Union to shift its weapons for the repulsion of aggression, for a retaliatory blow, to any other country, for instance Cuba."

While McCone nursed his doubts at Cap Ferrat, the CIA interrogation center at Opa-locka, Florida, sifted through hundreds upon hundreds of reports from Cuban refugees. Some claimed to have seen, before leaving Cuba, truck convoys hauling long, tubular objects, shrouded in tarpaulins. Others told of seeing missiles or rockets in place. Most were simple people, given to using simple words. The Spanish word most of them used was *cohete*. Its meaning is variable, stretching all the way from a child's firecracker to an intercontinental ballistic missile. When verification was possible, the long, tubular objects usually turned out to be more SAMs. The CIA, moreover, was becoming considerably disenchanted with refugees as a source of information. Too many of their reports, received and checked over the years since Castro seized power, had turned out to be politically motivated. The agency came to suspect that certain refugee leaders were in the business of manufacturing alarms, hoping that they could somehow draw the United States into war with Cuba and thus regain their homeland.

This was a job for professional spies, men with sufficient engineering or weapons experience to discriminate between air defense rockets and missiles capable of reaching beyond Cuba's shoreline to Florida, Puerto Rico, the Panama Canal and beyond. The CIA's own network of agents and subagents, which might have been counted upon for more professional reporting, had been decimated following the Bay of Pigs disaster. Castro's police and militia during the spring and summer of 1961 had launched a "war on traitors," arresting many thousands of Cubans suspected of sympathy for the United States. Among them were hundreds of CIA agents, now (in the technical term of the spying craft) "blown." Once this classical method of intelligence gathering had lost much of its importance for lack of trained agents the CIA fell back on the U-2 reconnaissance plane as its primary source of information.

The U-2 is a strange bird alongside modern airplanes built for more prosaic purposes. Its stubby fuselage is 49½ feet long, its tapering gliderlike wings stretch full 80 feet across. It can fly up to 4,000 miles at altitudes of 14 miles or better on less than 1,000 gallons of fuel. Its vision improves on the hawk's. Its

phenomenal cameras, aimed through seven port-
holes in the belly, can photograph a swath of earth
125 miles wide and 3,000 miles long. The photographs
come in 4,000 paired frames, each slightly overlapping
the other to produce a stereoscopic effect. The defini-
tion is remarkable. Photo interpreters studying the
developed and greatly enlarged pictures can without
much difficulty make out a newspaper headline eight
or ten miles below.

Carrying so much paraphernalia, the U-2 cannot be
burdened with landing gear. It takes off from a de-
tachable dolly. Coming back to ground, the wings are
shortened by bending each tip down. The pilot then
skids in along the reinforced belly of his plane, the
whole business resembling a South Sea island out-
rigger.

Until late August, the U-2 overflight schedule had
been limited to two flights a month. With the discovery
of the first SAM installation on August 29, the schedule
was stepped up. Between August 29 and October
7, seven U-2s were sent out to scan the island. Each
brought back more photographs of antiaircraft missiles, effective against high-flying airplanes but with
their slant range of 25 miles clearly no threat to the
United States.

Thus the President, at his news conference of September 13, again assured the country that the arms
shipments to Cuba "do not constitute a serious threat
to any other part of the hemisphere." He did not rule
out the possibility that the arms build-up might at
some future stage become such a threat. In fact, the
President carefully listed those bounds which, over-
stepped by the Communists, would force him to act:

If at any time the Communist buildup in Cuba
were to endanger or interfere with our security in any
way, including our base at Guantanamo, our passage
to the Panama Canal, our missile and space activities
at Cape Canaveral, or the lives of American citizens in

this country, or if Cuba should ever attempt to export
its aggressive purposes by forces or the threat of force
against any nation in this hemisphere, or become an
offensive military base of significant capacity for the
Soviet Union, then this country will do whatever must
be done to protect its own security and that of its allies.

McCone's warnings that the Russians might install
offensive missiles were not being ignored. The President, without the slightest ambiguity, had just served
notice on the Kremlin that he would act if Cuba were
to become "an offensive military base of significant
capacity for the Soviet Union." To assess the probabil-
ities of such a step, the Board of National Estimates
met in Washington on September 19. McCone was
still at Cap Ferrat, fretting and bombarding his deputy,
General Marshall S. Carter, with telegrams. President
Kennedy never saw the so-called honeymoon telegrams, sent on September 7, 10, 13, and 16. General
Carter did not distribute them outside the CIA. He
felt McCone had made plain his views before leaving
Washington. Having considered the McCone hypothesis and the available evidence, the Board prepared a
document, known as a National Intelligence Estimate,
conceding the possibility that the Russians might be
tempted to put missiles into Cuba, chiefly for the psychological effect of such a move throughout Latin
America. It also mentioned another possibility—that
Khrushchev might wish in this way to strengthen his
position in preparation for some new move against
Berlin. But its conclusion was negative. The Board held
that the establishment of a missile base in Cuba was
improbable for two reasons: first, because the Soviets
had reason to believe that the United States would react violently; second, because the Russians had been
extremely careful in the past not to station strategic
missiles outside their own territory, not even in other
Soviet-bloc countries. It seemed even less probable

that the Russians would entrust Castro with such dangerous weapons. The Board noted that Russia's air and sea communications to Cuba were long, hazardous and peculiarly vulnerable to American interdiction, that Castro's regime was inherently unstable, and that his recent adherence to the Soviet bloc had been self-proclaimed. There was no dissent.

From Cap Ferrat, McCone telegraphed General Carter the following day, September 20. He suggested most careful reconsideration of the National Intelligence Estimate on the ground that one element had been overlooked—the possibility that by planting offensive missiles in Cuba the Russians would greatly improve their bargaining position vis-à-vis the United States, for whatever use they cared to make of it.

On September 21, Ray Cline, deputy chief of intelligence at the CIA, received the first seemingly reliable eyewitness report from an agent in Cuba suggesting that missiles larger than the SAM had been delivered at dockside. The agent in question had seen a tailpiece of such a missile on a Cuban highway on September 12. He had sufficient technical grasp to estimate its circumference and to sketch its rear profile. The report had taken eight days to reach Opa-locka while the agent made his way out of Cuba as a refugee. Related evidence came to light at about the same time. Castro's pilot, evidently the worse for a hard night's drinking in Havana, had been heard to boast that Cuba no longer feared the United States because it now possessed long-range missiles with atomic warheads. "We will fight to the death," he said, "and perhaps we can win because we have everything, including atomic weapons." On October 3 came another report of unusual activity "probably connected with missiles" in Pinar del Río. Each of these scraps of information was distributed through the Government by the CIA, without raising the official temperature perceptibly.

The U-2 planes were being flown by Air Force officers who had been transferred to the CIA payroll, ostensibly as civilians, after a process of quasi-separation known in the trade as "sheep-dipping." They had overflown Cuba on September 5, 17, 26, 29, and October 5 and 7, without discovering anything beyond SAM sites, MIG fighter planes on various Cuban airfields, and Komar torpedo boats armed with short-range rockets. All but the September 5 flight, however, had limited their photographic sweeps to that portion of Cuba lying east of Havana. This was the result of a policy decision by the Committee on Overhead Reconnaissance (COMOR) meeting in McGeorge Bundy's office at the White House on September 10. Although the committee's very existence was a closely guarded secret, the reason it met that Monday in September was splashed all over the front pages of the newspapers. For the first time since Francis Gary Powers had been shot down over Russia on May 1, 1960, presumably the victim of a SAM such as the ones now being installed in western Cuba, another U-2, belonging to the Chinese Nationalists, had been destroyed in the air over the Chinese mainland on September 9. The astonishing speed of the SAM deployment west of Havana dictated a degree of caution. No man round the table in Bundy's office wanted to see another pilot lost or a fresh outcry raised round the world that might force the abandonment of future U-2 flights, thus denying to the United States its most reliable source of information. COMOR quickly agreed that the U-2 flights must continue, but decided to alter the flight pattern. Dean Rusk, the Secretary of State, suggested that instead of covering the whole island in a single flight (up one side of a line through the middle of the island, then back down the other), the flights should be shorter and more frequent, "dipping into" Cuban air space. By way of confusing the Cubans, Rusk also proposed a larger number of so-called peripheral flights that would peer into Cuba from beyond the three-mile limit.

McCone returned from his wedding trip to discover that western Cuba had not been overflown for a month. He promptly suggested, at a special conference on October 4, that the whole island be photographed at once with special attention to its western end. McCone recalls that several days were lost while various, less risky, alternatives were examined—among them the possibility of sending remote-controlled drone planes or balloons over the areas where SAMs were most likely to be in or near operational condition. The Administration's caution gave way when it became apparent that there was no ready substitute for the U-2. COMOR finally approved a flight plan on October 9, taking in an area of western Cuba beyond the range of the peripheral flights which had not been inspected from the air since September 5.

Colonel John Ralph Wright, Jr., of the Defense Intelligence Agency had studied the results of the September overflights with meticulous care. He was struck by the placement of SAMs, in an oddly trapezoidal pattern, near the Cuban town of San Cristóbal. This configuration roused Colonel Wright's suspicion. It resembled the placement of missile installations photographed repeatedly by pilots like Gary Powers over the Soviet Union. The colonel suggested to his boss, General Joseph Carroll, that San Cristóbal might be worth a closer look. Thus a look at San Cristóbal became part of the flight plan for the next U-2 sortie.

There was more delay due to cloud over the target area. The U-2 loses effectiveness when the sky is 25 per cent or more overcast. In addition, a day or two was lost while new Strategic Air Command pilots were checked out on U-2s built to CIA specifications. McNamara had suggested the shift to McCone in view of the greatly accelerated flight schedule. There was for the first time real danger of losing planes as well as pilots. In that situation, McNamara urged, Air Force regulars ought to take over. Some CIA people took this hard. General Carter, in McCone's month-long absence, had appealed to the White House, arguing that intelligence was properly the CIA's business and that it had its own control center to go with the planes, the trained pilots, and the experience. McGeorge Bundy dismissed the appeal.

By October 14, the skies over Cuba had cleared, the CIA had choked down its bitter pill and two Air Force pilots, thoroughly familiar by now with the CIA version of the U-2, had climbed into their borrowed flying machines. Both were Air Force majors—Rudolf Anderson, Jr., of Spartanburg, South Carolina, and Richard S. Heyser of Battle Creek, Michigan. Both had been born in 1927. Both had joined the Air Force in 1951. Both had served in the Far East—Anderson in Korea with the 15th Tactical Reconnaissance Squadron; Heyser in Japan.

As they entered the air space of western Cuba that Sunday, forewarned of possible ground fire, they were agreeably surprised to encounter none. They made their planned sweep of suspect areas, with San Cristóbal at the top of the list. Then they flew home, skidding in safely with the wings folded down at the tips to prevent ground looping. Their film magazines were quickly unloaded and transferred to a waiting jet for the flight to Washington. For Anderson and Heyser it had been an uneventful mission.

*So I decided that a quiet evening and a night
of sleep was the best preparation you could
have in the light of what you would face in
the days ahead.*
—McGEORGE BUNDY in a memorandum to
President Kennedy, March 4, 1963

No blare of trumpets announces a modern crisis. In
these matter-of-fact times, a telephone call will do.
Roswell Gilpatric, Deputy Secretary of Defense, was
in his Washington apartment at The Towers, dressing
for dinner, when the hot-line telephone from the Pentagon rang: the time, a few minutes after seven
o'clock. Lieutenant General Carroll, Chief of the Defense Intelligence Agency, wanted Gilpatric to know
that he had just seen something disturbing in the latest
U-2 photographs from Cuba. He was sending two men
in a military staff car with the evidence.

Gilpatric was knotting his tie when the two photo-
analysts walked into the bedroom. What they had to
show him were photographs of a field enclosed by
woods near San Cristóbal. The earth was scarred in a
four-slash pattern that intelligence men had seen
before only in the Soviet Union.

There were no ballistic missiles in sight that first
day. But a tent city appeared to be springing up near
a group of trucks and construction equipment. The
experienced photo-analysts had no difficulty picking
out missile erectors, launchers and transporters—all
of these inside the wider trapezoidal area that Colonel
Wright had remarked, with a SAM site at each corner

for protection. To a skilled interpreter of aerial photographs, thoroughly familiar with the vast U-2 port-
folio of medium-range missile sites on Soviet territory,
the evidence was compelling, if not yet conclusive.*

Gilpatric's first reaction was that the United States
and the Soviet Union stood at the beginning of a decisive confrontation. His second, that the President
could not be expected to tolerate a Soviet missile
base in Cuba. He directed General Carroll to check
the photographs more closely through the night. "Be
ready to brief the boss and the rest of us at seven-
thirty in the morning," he said. The "boss," Defense
Secretary McNamara, had left the Pentagon early that
evening to preside at one of those intellectual self-
improvement seminars known around Washington as
Hickory Hill University. This unique, informal gathering of New Frontiersmen took its name from their
customary meeting place, the home of Robert and
Ethel Kennedy in McLean, Virginia.

Gilpatric went on to dinner at the Fort McNair quarters of General Maxwell Taylor, chairman of the Joint
Chiefs of Staff. It was to have been a relaxed social
occasion, with music provided by an Army chorus.
General Carter of the CIA was there, also U. Alexis
Johnson, then Deputy Under Secretary of State, and
General Carroll. As the evening wore on, each of the
principal guests was called to the telephone for quick,
whispered discussions with colleagues or subordi-
nates. Each returned in silence, trapped in private

* In June 1963, Colonel Wright's crucial contribution was
acknowledged with the award of an Oak Leaf Cluster to the
Legion of Merit he had received ten years earlier. The cita-
tion reads, in part: "He performed a unique service to his
country by singlehandedly analyzing a series of intelligence
reports concerning the activities of the Soviet Union in Cuba
and, by this analysis, pinpointing the location of the first
medium-range ballistic missiles deployed by the USSR in
the Western hemisphere. His analysis led him to recommend
for immediate coverage by high-altitude reconnaissance aircraft the exact location which was photographed on 14th
October, 1962, and revealed the existence of those missiles in
Cuba."

thought about Russian missiles in Cuba and the decisions that would have to be taken tomorrow. There were too many outsiders in the room, wives included, for a general discussion on the meaning of Khrushchev's secret stroke. The ladies present were the first of several dozen government wives who in the days ahead would find the behavior of their husbands curious to the point of eccentricity.

McCone, the Administration's Cassandra, had left Washington at three o'clock that afternoon to deal with a personal tragedy. Paul J. Pigott, the son of Mrs. McCone, had been killed in a California sports-car accident. The CIA chief was on his way to Los Angeles and from there to Seattle, escorting the body of young Pigott.

In McCone's absence, General Carter was the first to receive word of the San Cristóbal discovery from the photo-analysts at the National Photographic Interpretation Center. Here the U-2 film had been developed and minutely scanned, frame by frame, with the help of elaborate magnifying and stereoscopic instruments. It was Carter who alerted General Carroll. McGeorge Bundy, President Kennedy's special assistant for national security affairs, was the usual channel to the White House. He got the news at 8:30 P.M., also by telephone, from another CIA man, deputy director Ray Cline. Bundy was at home that evening, giving a dinner for Charles E. Bohlen, the newly appointed Ambassador to France. Among the guests were members of the French Embassy and at least one Washington reporter. "It was clear to me that we were in a major crisis," Bundy recalls. McCone's hypothesis that Khrushchev might install missiles in Cuba had seemed to him less than convincing so long as the Government had no evidence more reliable than the mass of confused, contradictory refugee reports. The faith of the analysts in their photographs had now dissolved Bundy's doubts.

Bundy briefly considered and dismissed the idea of

telling the President that night; then calling an immediate White House conference to consider the new situation. The President had been out campaigning the previous day. He had returned to Washington at almost two o'clock Monday morning looking worn after campaign appearances in Niagara Falls and New York City. Bundy felt there was nothing the President could do that was not already being done except to lose a night's sleep. His dinner guests represented another obstacle. Washington was a gossipy town. To walk out on his own dinner party would certainly have started tongues wagging. "The President," Bundy felt, "would have asked the inevitable question: 'Is the evidence hard enough to go on?' He would have asked us to double check everything, to order more photographs. These in any case had already been ordered. I decided the bad news could wait till Tuesday morning." *

Another, more formal dinner was in progress at that hour under the glittering crystal chandeliers of the eighth-floor dining room in the State Department. The chandeliers—a gift from Douglas Dillon, the Wall Street banker who had served President Eisenhower as Ambassador to France and Under Secretary of State before he joined the Kennedy Administration as Secretary of the Treasury—caught the candlelight from the long table below as Secretary of State Dean Rusk chatted with his guest, Foreign Minister Gerhard Schroeder of West Germany. Paul Nitze, then Assistant Secretary of Defense for International Security Affairs,

---

* Months after the missiles crisis, a national magazine raised the question whether any White House assistant had the authority to keep information of comparable gravity from the President. Only then, in March 1963, did Kennedy ask Bundy: "Why didn't you tell me that night?" Bundy explained, in a memorandum dated March 4, that he had seen nothing to be gained by burdening the President until the information had been rechecked most carefully. He added: "So I decided that a quiet evening and a night of sleep were the best preparation you could have in light of what you would face in the days ahead."

was sitting beside another German official, discussing a possible new Russian squeeze on Berlin. He noticed Rusk excuse himself and leave the table. A waiter had handed the Secretary of State a note, calling him to the telephone in the butler's pantry. The caller, Roger Hilsman, gave Rusk the facts in elliptical fashion.

"Do you, personally, think this is it?" the Secretary of State asked.

"There has been only a preliminary analysis," Hilsman replied, "but from what I can get over the phone there doesn't seem to be much doubt."

Rusk returned to the dinner table and calmly resumed his conversation with Schroeder about matters far removed from Cuba: the future of NATO, the European Common Market, Berlin, and what the Western Allies should do if Khrushchev made good his repeated threat to provoke a new Berlin crisis soon after the American election. At the first opportunity, however, Rusk drew Nitze aside, led him to the handsome terrace alongside the state dining room overlooking the Lincoln Memorial, and told him what he had just heard from Hilsman.

"We discussed the alternatives quietly, so the Germans would not hear," Nitze recalls. "The President had already said we would not tolerate the installation of offensive missiles in Cuba. We both knew that the Pentagon had prepared contingency plans for an invasion or an air strike. Suddenly the contingency had become a fact. We both felt that either plan, in execution, would have grave and perhaps unpredictable consequences round the world. We could expect the British to take a different view. The Allies generally had failed to appreciate why the presence of missiles in Cuba—if it came to that—would be intolerable to the United States. We found it hard to imagine that the Russians would not respond by moving against Iran or Berlin, even Vietnam. We, therefore, agreed that the United States must move with deliberation, not merely proceed with existing contingency plans."

While Rusk and Nitze rejoined their German guests for coffee and brandy, Roger Hilsman was at his home in Chevy Chase, Maryland, telephoning other high officials of the State Department. He passed on the bare facts to the Under Secretary of State, George Ball; then tracked down the man most immediately concerned, Edwin M. Martin, Assistant Secretary of State for Inter-American Affairs. Martin was at the National Press Club, addressing a dinner of the journalism society Sigma Delta Chi. What he was saying—at the moment Hilsman called—had been said before by the President himself. Yes, it was true, Martin said, the Russians were building a network of antiaircraft missile sites in Cuba, they also had rocket-launching torpedo boats, late-model MIG fighter planes, and some 5,000 Soviet technicians on the ground. All this was so, Martin conceded, but the Administration saw no threat from Cuba. "This military build-up is basically defensive in character," Martin said, "and would not add more than a few hours to the time required to invade Cuba successfully should that become necessary. Of course, any individual weapon is offensive if you are on the other end of it; but, taken together, the present military capabilities in Cuba would not materially increase the Cuban ability to undertake offensive action outside the island."

Martin was in midspeech when Hilsman called the Press Club. A State Department aide from Martin's bureau of Inter-American affairs asked: "Is it urgent enough to interrupt?"

Hilsman replied: "For God's sake, no! But it is important enough to have him call me when he's finished —so long as it doesn't attract attention."

As soon as Martin was through speaking and responding to questions, he went into a telephone booth, on the excuse of telling his wife to expect him at home in a few minutes. From Hilsman he learned that the unthinkable had happened, making instant nonsense of the assurances he had just repeated in good faith to the assembled membership of Sigma Delta Chi's Washington professional chapter.

In hindsight it seems obvious that the Administration should have anticipated the installation of Soviet missiles in Cuba. That it failed to do so is not the fault of any individual. The failure can be traced instead to a state of mind, an unwillingness to believe that Khrushchev would do anything so preposterous. Perhaps the crucial error on the American side was the belief at middle and senior levels of the Administration that Khrushchev, being a rational man, would not take a step that seemed to Americans so dangerously irrational. On the Russian side, the crucial failure lay in grossly underestimating President Kennedy's readiness to act when challenged.

Roberta Wohlstetter has pointed out, in a study comparing the Cuban missiles crisis with Pearl Harbor, that the Japanese made the same mistake. "We underestimated the risks that the Japanese were willing to take in 1941 and the risks that Khrushchev was willing to take in the summer and fall of 1962," Mrs. Wohlstetter reminds us. "Both the Russians and the Japanese, for their part, underestimated our ultimate willingness to respond." *

Although Khrushchev has since been deposed and denounced, without specification, for "harebrained scheming," the Soviet public has been told nothing about the most dangerously harebrained of all his miscalculations, the Cuban missiles ploy. What led him to believe that it could succeed? John McCone believes that the United States led the Russians into that frame of mind by a whole series of things it had done—or failed to do. Kennedy, for example, let them get away with building the Berlin wall. He allowed the Bay of Pigs landing to fail. McCone blames not only the Ken-

* Roberta Wohlstetter, "Cuba and Pearl Harbor: Hindsight and Foresight." Rand Corporation memorandum, April 1965.

nedy Administration but also the Eisenhower Administration before it for creating a "climate of inaction."

There is reason to believe that Khrushchev took Kennedy's measure at their Vienna meeting in June 1961,
and decided this was a young man who would shrink
from hard decisions. The President's youth troubled
Khrushchev, as he later confided to an American visitor. Kennedy had given permission for the CIA to
launch a quixotic landing attempt in Cuba, putting
some 1,500 exiles ashore in the wrong place at the
wrong time without sufficient ammunition or promise
of reinforcements, and then (perhaps absurdly, as
Khrushchev looked at the world) acknowledged full
personal responsibility for the failure.

There is no evidence to support the belief that Khrushchev ever questioned America's power. He questioned only the President's readiness to use it. As he
once told Robert Frost, he came to believe that Americans are "too liberal to fight." Khrushchev must have
known—even if Kennedy did not, when he stumped
the country in 1960 talking of a "missile gap"—that no
missile gap existed. Thanks in large part to the reve-
lations of Colonel Oleg Penkovskiy, perhaps the most
remarkable secret agent of the cold war, Kennedy was
to discover only after he took office that the United
States possessed vastly more power to destroy the
Soviet Union than the other way around. The fact that
the President was unwilling to use even a tiny frac-
tion of that power to topple Castro must have impressed Khrushchev. His own nerve had not failed
when it became necessary to send tanks into Budapest
on November 4, 1956, to throttle the revolution and
to murder Imre Nagy for presuming to take Hungary
out of the Soviet bloc. President Eisenhower had not
lifted a finger, for all the brave promises about liberat-
ing Eastern Europe written into the Republican
platform by John Foster Dulles. Now Kennedy had
not lifted a finger to crush Castro, whose regime must
have been every bit as repugnant to Kennedy as the

Nagy regime had been repugnant to Khrushchev. Khrushchev may have reflected: the Americans certainly possess overwhelming power—but they have forgotten how a great power must behave.

At Vienna Khrushchev had bullied Kennedy over the Bay of Pigs defeat. Kennedy called it a mistake. Khrushchev kept prodding for an explanation to the point of exasperating the President, who repeated his confession of error, then snapped: "Don't you ever make mistakes in your country, Mr. Chairman?" Khrushchev agreed that mistakes had indeed been made in the history of the Soviet state and had been courageously acknowledged, just as the President acknowledged his mistakes. Khrushchev was alluding, of course, to his own secret speech before the Twentieth Party Congress in 1956, when he denounced Stalin as a murderous tyrant. Kennedy did not see fit to remind Khrushchev that it required rather less courage to saddle a dead man with all the crimes of his era than to confess one's own failures.

James Reston saw Kennedy ten minutes after his final meeting with Khrushchev. He remembers it this way:

He [the President] came into a dim room in the American Embassy shaken and angry. He had tried, as always, to be calm and rational with Khrushchev, to get him to define what the Soviet Union would and would not do, and Khrushchev had bullied him and threatened him with war over Berlin.

We will have to know much more about that confrontation between Kennedy and Khrushchev, one now deprived of life and the other of power, before we can be sure, but Kennedy said just enough in that room in the embassy to convince me of the following:

Khrushchev had studied the events of the Bay of Pigs; he would have understood if Kennedy had left Castro alone or destroyed him; but when Kennedy was rash enough to strike at Cuba but not bold enough to finish the job, Khrushchev decided he was

dealing with an inexperienced young leader who
could be intimidated and blackmailed. The Communist decision to put offensive missiles into Cuba
was the final gamble of this assumption.*

The President returned from Vienna, by way of
London, brooding about one defeat after another, and
extraordinarily sensitive to any unnecessary talk about
nuclear war. Yet a new Berlin crisis was brewing.
Khrushchev had delivered an ultimatum in Vienna.
And the Western Allies, notably the Germans, seemed
to require reassurance that they would not be left to
fend for themselves. In a news conference held on the
day the President returned from London, Roswell Gilpatric gave a public undertaking that if Europe was
about to be overwhelmed by Soviet power, the United
States would not flinch from the use of nuclear weapons. This was no revelation but a timely restatement
of long-established policy. Nevertheless, the President
angrily telephoned Gilpatric that night to reproach
him for talking too much. Next morning, he called
again—to apologize. Kennedy explained that the Vienna encounter had left him tired and irritable. Some
weeks afterward, Gilpatric was invited to address the
Business Council, a blue-ribbon panel of industrialists,
bankers and merchants, at its October meeting in Hot
Springs, Virginia. He decided that the time had come
to bury the missile-gap fallacy by making a public disclosure of America's total armed strength and
Russia's comparative weakness. Dean Rusk, Bundy,
and the President himself cleared the speech text. All
agreed it was time to let the world know the facts,
and that it was better done by Gilpatric than by a
headline figure such as Rusk or McNamara. Gilpatric's
arithmetic of strike and counter-strike could scarcely
have surprised Khrushchev. No nation on earth had
been more reckless with military secrets than the

* The New York Times Magazine, November 15, 1964.

United States. Missile manufacturers bought full-page advertisements in glossy magazines to boast of the installations they had just put in, with place names and photographs supplied. It may well have shaken the Soviet leaders to discover that the United States had managed, through U-2 overflights and otherwise, to pinpoint exact missile locations and numbers inside the Soviet Union, as if no Iron Curtain existed.* They could be sure that each of the Soviet missile sites was now the target of an American missile. There is reason to believe that Khrushchev in the months that followed had to face pressing demands from his own military chiefs for a bigger, more reliable, better hardened Soviet ICBM force and that he turned them down. For years he had been juggling Russia's limited resources, trying to better the standard of living, and to build more apartments in the overcrowded cities where two and sometimes three families had to share a kitchen and bathroom; while at the same time dis-

---

* In his Hot Springs speech on October 21, 1961, Gilpatric said: "Our confidence in our ability to deter Communist action, or resist Communist blackmail, is based upon a sober appreciation of the relative military power of the two sides. We doubt that the Soviet leadership has in fact any less realistic views, although this may not be always apparent from their extravagant claims. . . . Their Iron Curtain is not so impenetrable as to force us to accept at face value the Kremlin's boasts." The United States, Gilpatric specified, possessed 600 intercontinental heavy bombers and many more medium bombers which could reach Soviet targets by refueling in flight; in addition to "dozens" of intercontinental ballistic missiles and six Polaris submarines at sea, each carrying 16 missiles. "The total number of our nuclear delivery vehicles, tactical as well as strategic, is in the tens of thousands; and, of course, we have more than one warhead for each vehicle," he stated. This meant that the Soviets would be inviting destruction if they dared to mount a sneak attack on the United States. "The destructive power which the United States could bring to bear even after a Soviet surprise attack upon our forces would be as great as—perhaps greater than —the total undamaged forces which the enemy can threaten to launch against the United States in a first strike," Gilpatric said. "In short, we have a second-strike capability which is at least as extensive as what the Soviets can deliver by striking first."

pensing aid to India, Egypt, Indonesia, and other developing nations, keeping Eastern Europe firmly in hand, fighting a new cold war with China, and wrestling with the unsolved riddle of how to grow more wheat in Russia without dismantling the collective farm system. Unlike the American President's chronic problem of finding ways to give away the country's permanent economic surplus, Khrushchev's was the problem of rationing permanent scarcity. It may be that the Cuban missiles ploy appealed to Khrushchev for these economic reasons. It was certainly cheaper to put existing medium-range and intermediate-range missiles into Cuba than to embark on a new ICBM crash program that would run into many billions of rubles. It had the merit of answering Castro's clamor for help against the American invaders he kept seeing on the horizon. And it would give Russia the kind of leverage she had never before enjoyed—a strategic base only 90 miles from the United States. There were risks, of course. The Soviet marshals almost certainly pointed them out to Khrushchev. But he knew Kennedy; they did not. And he must have felt confident that Kennedy would do nothing more than protest, raise an uproar in the U.N., and in the end accept them. The thought that no American President—Republican or Democrat, young or old —could in fact have submitted to this direct intrusion of Soviet power into the hemisphere evidently escaped Khrushchev's notice or that of his advisers.

Why did Kennedy and his Administration seem to ignore, or downgrade, the fragments of information available before October 14? A likely factor was his "once-burned, twice-shy" attitude toward the CIA and the Joint Chiefs of Staff. The Bay of Pigs adventure had taught him to be skeptical of the professionals. He had once believed the solemn assurances of Allen Dulles that Cuba would be easier than Guatemala. While valuing McCone for his unassailable position on Capitol Hill and his services as the Administration's go-between with Eisenhower, Kennedy had not overcome his reservations about the quality of intelligence the agency was providing to him.

The Congressional election campaign then in progress had another, more important bearing on the President's state of mind. The Republicans had made of Cuba their central campaign issue, taxing Kennedy with a do-nothing policy. This gave them a vested interest in exaggerating the case, throwing the Administration back on the defensive. When Senator Keating, on October 10, claimed to have "100 per cent reliable" information that six intermediate-range missile sites were under construction in Cuba, the Administration possessed no such hard evidence. All it had were two unverified refugee reports about a single site at Remedios. In retrospect, Keating was almost certainly justified in drawing attention to the Soviet arms build-up, with all its perilous implications, even if he was wrong on details. As an Opposition Senator he was free to make play with refugee reports. The Government needed solid proof before it could act. Lacking that proof, the Administration started by denouncing the Republican critics for irresponsibility and soon developed a vested interest in discounting the evidence.

Taking full advantage of hindsight, it is clear that the Administration should have recognized sooner the importance of the September 21 report concerning a new missile a good deal larger than the SAM. Roger Hilsman has pointed to another classic instance of hard evidence overlooked or not given sufficient weight because it did not fit the Administration's preconceptions at the time: Two of the Soviet ships delivering arms to Cuba that summer were the freighters *Omsk* and *Poltava*. Both had exceptionally wide hatches. They had been built for the Soviet lumber trade. Their decks were loaded with trucks, suggesting some kind of bulk cargo below decks. American reconnaissance did not fail to observe that both ships rode high in the water, higher than they should have ridden if they were carrying bulk cargo. They arrived in Cuba on September 8 and 15 respectively. The intelligence community assumed at first that wide-hatch lumber ships had been pressed into service for no other reason than a general scarcity of bottoms. Not until the discovery of 60-foot missiles at San Cristóbal did American intelligence grasp the significance of *Omsk* and *Poltava* riding so high in the water, their extra-wide hatches sealed. Only then did Washington recognize that the ships rode high because their hatch covers concealed "a space-consuming cargo such as an MRBM," to quote McNamara, instead of bulk cargo. In short, before it could properly evaluate the clues that Soviet MRBMs might be going into Cuba, the Administration had to free itself of the fixed idea that Khrushchev would never be so foolish as to put them there. The awakening came abruptly on Monday, October 15.

*A missile is a missile. It makes no great dif-
ference whether you are killed by a missile
fired from the Soviet Union or from Cuba.*
—ROBERT S. MCNAMARA, October 16, 1962

ALL NIGHT LONG a team of intelligence specialists was
at work, checking and cross-checking the eagle's eye-
view of San Cristóbal while the unsuspecting President slept. At 7:30 that morning Secretary McNamara
examined the evidence put before him by General
Carroll. The four-slash pattern bore an ominous resem-
blance to the configuration of Soviet missile sites. But
the Secretary of Defense, noting the absence of missiles, felt that the evidence at this early stage was not
hard enough to warrant alerting the President. Mc-
George Bundy, whose direct responsibility it was to
keep Kennedy informed, had resolved his own doubts.
At eight o'clock, in his little basement office at the
White House, Bundy met with an intelligence officer
and two photo-analysts. He studied the photographs
and the accompanying intelligence report, then took
the elevator to the Kennedy living quarters. He found
the President sitting on the edge of his bed, in pa-
jamas and dressing gown, looking at the morning newspapers.

Kennedy was a quick, omnivorous reader. He now
started issuing instructions about various matters,
spiced with personal comments on the headlines of the

day. Bundy allowed himself to interrupt. "Mr. President," he said, "there is now hard photographic evidence, which you will see a little later, that the Russians have offensive missiles in Cuba." There is no record of President Kennedy's immediate response. Bundy recalls that he lost no time fumbling. The President's principal concern was to make certain that the information was accurate beyond challenge. In a preliminary way he speculated about the choices confronting the United States. He then directed Bundy to call an extraordinary meeting, in strictest secrecy, for 11:45 that morning. While Bundy made notes, the President dictated who should be there: Vice President Johnson, Secretary of State Rusk, Secretary of Defense McNamara, Attorney General Robert Kennedy, General Maxwell Taylor, General Carter, Roswell Gilpatric, George Ball, Edwin Martin, Bundy himself, Ted Sorensen, Douglas Dillon, Ambassador Bohlen, and Kenneth O'Donnell, the President's appointments secretary. "He wanted to play it very close," Bundy recalls.

The President kept all his scheduled appointments that first day. At 9:30 he welcomed astronaut Walter Schirra, Jr., with Mrs. Schirra and their two children. He chatted with them, showing no outward sign of strain. To the Schirras' twelve-year-old son he presented a tie clasp in the shape of his World War II PT boat 109, to their daughter a new chain bracelet. Then he led the astronaut's family out on the White House lawn to inspect his daughter Caroline's grazing pony, Macaroni. It was important to keep up appearances.

Dean Rusk—after a preliminary discussion in his own office with Under Secretary Ball, Deputy Under Secretary Johnson, Assistant Secretary Martin, and Roger Hilsman—left the State Department at ten o'clock to meet a state visitor, the Crown Prince of Libya, at the airport. At nine o'clock that same morning the U.S. Ambassador to the United Nations, Adlai Stevenson, left New York on an Eastern Air Lines shuttle flight to attend a White House luncheon honoring the Libyan prince.

Between appointments that Tuesday morning the President telephoned his brother at the Justice Department. Robert Kennedy expressed surprise and concern upon hearing the news. "I had no doubt we were moving into a serious crisis," he recalls. The President also spoke by telephone with John J. McCloy in New York. McCloy, a Republican lawyer with banking connections, had occupied a succession of important offices under Democratic Presidents. He had been Assistant Secretary of War under Roosevelt, High Commissioner to Germany under Truman, and, in the early months of the Kennedy Administration, he had helped lobby for Congressional support to establish the Arms Control and Disarmament Agency. McCloy was about to leave for Europe on a business trip, but he would be back in a few days. He told the President he recommended drastic action to get the missiles out of Cuba.

Dean Rusk, meanwhile, was seeking advice from his old boss, former Secretary of State Dean Acheson. "The information was still sketchy," Acheson recalls. "I felt we would need to know more before we could frame a decision. It was obvious, however, that time would be the essential factor. We would have to choose between the risk of eliminating the weapons and the risk of allowing sufficient time for them to become operative. I felt the latter risk was worth taking."

The group that assembled in the Cabinet Room at 11:45 that morning later came to be known as the Executive Committee of the National Security Council. It had no formal existence until October 22, although it met two and often three times a day that first week in total secrecy. Vice President Lyndon Johnson was there *ex officio*. Rusk, McNamara, General Taylor, and McCone (when he returned from Seattle) represented the Government departments chiefly concerned

—the State and Defense Departments, the Joint Chiefs of Staff, the Central Intelligence Agency. The rest were individuals whose names the President had dictated to Bundy upon first hearing the news because he had come to trust and rely upon their judgment: his brother, the Attorney General; Roswell Gilpatric, who had won the President's respect as a member of special task forces concerned with counter-insurgency and Southeast Asian problems; George Ball, Gilpatric's counterpart at the State Department; Dillon, the only survivor of the Eisenhower Administration; the President's chief assistants—Bundy, Sorensen, and O'Donnell; Charles (Chip) Bohlen, former Ambassador to Moscow, personal friend and chief interpreter of the mysterious goings-on behind the Kremlin wall. Bohlen was about to leave for his new Embassy in Paris. Llewellyn Thompson, just returned from Moscow, took his place. There were notable omissions. The President had never been comfortable in the larger, more formal sessions of the National Security Council, whose membership was stipulated by an Act of Congress. He called few Cabinet meetings, on the theory that the Postmaster General or the Secretary of Interior, having nothing to contribute to foreign policy decisions, ought to use their time more profitably improving mail services or beautifying the national parks. After the disaster at the Bay of Pigs in April 1961, Kennedy had started creating special committees to study and report on specific problems. He set up task forces on Berlin, on counter-insurgency, and on Southeast Asia. The Executive Committee, in effect, was another, larger, task force. It had the virtue of flexibility. Dean Acheson, for example, though a lawyer in private practice, had been a member of the Berlin task force. Before long he was to become involved also in the missiles crisis deliberations upon the President's invitation.

That first Tuesday session was dominated by somber reflections concerning the nature of the challenge from Moscow. Everyone round the table understood that a precipitate response might aggravate the situation, perhaps irreparably, but that to do nothing about the missiles in Cuba could be more dangerous still.

The first reading was that Khrushchev, after fifteen months of talk about forcing a Berlin settlement on his own terms, was about to act. As soon as the American elections were past, he would probably go to the United Nations General Assembly, unveil his rocket batteries in Cuba and put his proposition: let the Western powers get out of Berlin in exchange for the removal of Soviet missiles in Cuba. An alternative theory, rejecting the analogy between Cuba and Berlin, was that Khrushchev might be preparing to trade off the Cuban missiles for the American Jupiters based in Turkey and Italy. Llewellyn Thompson's immediate reaction, like Bohlen's, was to blame himself for having misread the portents. "I just didn't believe the Russians would do it," he recalls. "They had never trusted their own satellites with missiles. Though once the missiles were there my immediate reaction was to relate it to Khrushchev's repeated assurances that he would do nothing about Berlin until after our election. I figured he was planning to come to the U.N. with those blue chips in his pocket."

Either way, whether the Russian goal was to incorporate Berlin into East Germany or to force the Jupiter bases out of Europe, the alternatives for the United States were ugly. If the President did nothing, the Soviets would certainly succeed in exposing the hollowness of the Monroe Doctrine and the Rio Treaty, indeed of all United States treaty commitments to use its great power in defense of smaller nations anywhere. "To the Latins, Khrushchev would have looked like a winner," one State Department official said. Douglas Dillon recalls: "The first reaction of the President and the others, in full agreement, was that we simply could not accept the fact of Soviet missiles in Cuba trained on the United States. Everyone round the table recognized that we were in a major crisis. We didn't know, that day, if the country would come through it with Washington intact."

Kennedy's first decision was to order a sharp increase in the number of U-2 overflights. Instead of two flights a week, twenty would take place during the next six days. The second decision was that there must be no disclosure concerning the presence of Soviet missiles in Cuba until the President had decided what to do about them. Only then would he announce the frightening facts, if possible at the moment of telling the world what steps he was taking to remove them. Kennedy meant to control events, not to be swept along by them. The political initiative was to be his alone. The President's decision would await the results of fresh overflights giving a truer dimension of the danger from Cuba. He cautioned the Executive Committee members to tell their wives and secretaries nothing. Only those with a demonstrated "need to know" were to see intelligence reports. At one point during the tense days that followed, senior officials were doing their own typing. "Some of my own basic papers were done in my own handwriting," Dean Rusk said to an interviewer after the crisis, "in order to limit the possibility of further spread."

Adlai Stevenson first heard about the missiles from the President himself, immediately after the 1 P.M. luncheon for the Libyan crown prince. Kennedy showed his U.N. Ambassador the photographic evidence when the two were alone together. "We'll have to do something quickly," the President said. "I suppose the alternatives are to go in by air and wipe them out, or to take other steps to render the weapons inoperable." Stevenson replied: "Let's not go to an air strike until we have explored the possibilities of a peaceful solution." * The President urged Stevenson to remain in Washington for several days and to join a crisis conference at the State Department that afternoon involving Rusk, Ball, Martin, Alexis Johnson, Bohlen, and Thompson. Before leaving, Stevenson urged the President not to cancel any of his scheduled campaign appearances round the country. "That would give alarm," he warned. Kennedy agreed.

In Moscow that day, Nikita Khrushchev sent for the new American Ambassador, Foy Kohler. The Soviet leader had just returned from his vacation retreat at Gagra on the Black Sea coast. Kohler found him in a genial mood, fairly brimming with assurances of goodwill toward the United States. Khrushchev said he understood that Fidel Castro's September 25 announcement concerning the establishment of a major port in Cuba for the Soviet Union's Atlantic fishing fleet had caused the President political trouble at home. He told Kohler the announcement should not and would not have been made, except that he was out of Moscow at the time. Soviet purposes in Cuba were, as everyone knew, wholly defensive. Would the Ambassador please make clear in his report that the last thing Khrushchev wanted was to cause the President any embarrassment on the very eve of national elections? It seems obvious that Khrushchev's purpose was to buy time until his missile bases were in working order. He could not have known that by the time Kohler's report reached the President it would have been discredited as one more piece of a carefully planned deception. Dobrynin had given similar assur-

---

* In March 1965, four months before his death, Stevenson recalled: "I was a little alarmed that Kennedy's first consideration should have been the air strike. I told him that sooner or later we would have to go to the U.N. and it was vitally important we go there with a reasonable case."

ances to Robert Kennedy, and also to Chester Bowles on October 13. While there may be some reason to believe that Dobrynin had no knowledge of missiles in Cuba, Khrushchev certainly knew the truth.* He was lying and the President knew it.

That first day's crisis discussions amounted, in Dean Rusk's phrase, to "boxing the compass." The entire spectrum of possible American responses was reviewed. "Everybody gave his offhand reaction," Gilpatric recalls. "There was a lot of tactical thinking aloud. The discussion went round and round without a beginning or an end." Only the setting changed as the President's counselors shifted from the White House to the State Department in the afternoon, then back to the White House at 6:30 P.M.

There were disagreements about the military effect of Khrushchev's move. McNamara, at the outset and for at least two days afterward, dissented from the view that the Russians were trying to force an abrupt change in the strategic balance between East and West. "A missile is a missile," he said. "It makes no great difference whether you are killed by a missile fired from the Soviet Union or from Cuba."

The Secretary of Defense argued that the Soviet Union already possessed intercontinental ballistic missiles capable of hitting the United States from Russia itself, and would go on building more of them, whatever happened in Cuba. As he saw it, the only military effect would be to reduce America's warning time in the event of war by just a few minutes. He came to concede, however, that even if the effect on the strategic balance was relatively small, the political effect in Latin America and elsewhere would be large. McNamara seemingly ignored the possibility that Rus-

---

* To this day, Robert Kennedy credits the Soviet Ambassador with sincerity. He believes that Dobrynin was misled by his own government, presumably acting on the sound principle that any ambassador's denials sound more convincing if he does not know the whole truth.

sia's intercontinental missiles may have been less numerous, also less accurate, than American intelligence assumed them to be. Thus he dismissed the possibility that the Russians might have sneaked comparatively short-range missiles into Cuba because they were looking for a quick, relatively cheap way of righting the balance temporarily.

It was precisely this reasoning that had prompted the United States—with NATO approval—to put Jupiter missiles into Turkey and Italy five years earlier, at the height of the Sputnik hysteria. At that time the United States possessed no reliable intercontinental missile system. McNamara's estimate of Soviet ICBM strength seems grossly inflated when compared with this 1962 report to Allied intelligence from Colonel Penkovskiy:

Khrushchev boasts that we are ready, we have everything. This is just so much idle talk. He himself probably does not see the whole picture. *As far as launching a planned missile attack to destroy definite targets is concerned, we are not yet capable of doing it. We simply do not have any missiles that are accurate enough.*

According to information acquired from [Chief Marshal of Artillery Sergey Sergeyevitch] Varentsov and others, many of our big missiles are still on the drawing boards, in the prototype stage, or are still undergoing tests. There are altogether no more than a few dozen of these, instead of the "shower" of missiles with which Khrushchev has been threatening the West. . . . At the moment we have a certain number of missiles with nuclear warheads capable of reaching the United States or South America but these are single missiles, not in mass production, and they are far from perfect. . . .*

---

* From *The Penkovskiy Papers* by Oleg Penkovskiy, translated by Peter Deryabin. Copyright © 1965 by Doubleday & Company, Inc. Reprinted by permission of the publisher.

Among those who disagreed was Paul Nitze, once head of the State Department policy planning staff and at the time one of McNamara's assistant secretaries. Nitze had joined the discussions after the opening session with the President. He felt that the presence of missiles in Cuba exposed a large part of the American strategic bomber force, based in the Southeastern states, to sudden attack on the ground. The warning time would be cut from fifteen minutes to two or three minutes.

The essential disagreement between McNamara and Nitze, in trying to gauge the degree of danger, put them on opposite sides of the argument about how the President should respond. Those who felt "the fat was in the fire," as Dillon put it, called for an air strike to remove the missile bases by force. In the beginning, this group included General Taylor, Nitze, and Dillon. McCone was to join them on the following day.

The opponents of direct armed action at this stage were McNamara, Ball, and Gilpatric. Vice President Johnson listened, seldom speaking unless spoken to. As for Dean Rusk, he withheld his own views that first day and for several days to come. McGeorge Bundy was later to change his position, but that first day he argued for a diplomatic approach. Ambassador Thompson, just returned from Moscow, knew Khrushchev better than any other American. When asked to anticipate the Russian leader's reaction, he recommended against an air attack. The missile bases were Soviet-manned and bombing them meant killing Russians. Thompson warned that Khrushchev could react impulsively, perhaps triggering a world war.

Late Tuesday afternoon, some 500 editorial writers, radio and television commentators, attending a foreign policy conference at the State Department, heard the President ruminate—off the record—on the hazards of living in the thermonuclear age. "I don't think it is unfair to say that the United States—and the world—

is now passing through one of its most critical periods," Kennedy said. "And it may be that it will continue to pass through a period of comparable criticality for the next few months—maybe years. . . . Our major problem, over all, is the survival of our country, the protection of its vital interests without . . . the beginning of the third and perhaps the last war. That is the decade we live in. And that is the burden all of us bear. It is rather ironical that the two strongest countries in the world, the Soviet Union and the United States, are the two countries which today live in the greatest danger."

The President gave no sign that the very words he used—"critical," "survival," "vital interests," "greatest danger," words worn smooth by endless repetition over the years—had for him taken on a terrifying new meaning that morning. Only at the close of his remarks did Kennedy betray his inward feeling of standing alone to face some unknown danger. He recited to the molders of American public opinion a wry little poem:

> *Bullfight critics row on row*
> *Crowd the enormous plaza de toros,*
> *But only one is there who knows,*
> *And he is the one who fights the bull.**

It was 4:52 Tuesday afternoon when he hurried out of the State Department auditorium. He left his critics laughing.

That evening the President slipped away from the White House to attend the last in a round of farewell parties for Chip and Avis Bohlen, this one at the Georgetown home of the Washington columnist, Joseph Alsop. Kennedy had come to lean heavily on

---

* From *Oxford Addresses on Poetry* by Robert Graves. Copyright © 1961, 1962 by International Authors NV. Reprinted by permission of Doubleday & Company, Inc.

Bohlen's understanding of Soviet affairs during the first twenty-two months of his Presidency. Reluctant to see Bohlen leave Washington in a moment of grave danger, the President led the Ambassador into the Alsop garden for a long private talk. The matter of delaying Bohlen's departure for Paris had already been raised with Dean Rusk, who argued that a postponement now would destroy any prospect of keeping the crisis under wraps until the President had determined his course of action. Too many people in Paris—and in Moscow—would ask questions. When it was time to say good-bye, Mrs. Bohlen shook the President's hand. "Well, Mr. President, we'll be off in the morning," she said. Kennedy, still unreconciled to Bohlen's departure, replied: "I wouldn't be too sure about his leaving."

*I have enjoyed that warm reception I've got-
ten from my fellow Elis as I drove into the
city. But they will learn, as this country has
learned, that the Democratic Party is best for
them as it is for the country.*
—JOHN F. KENNEDY speaking in New Haven,
October 17, 1962

THE PRESIDENT kept a promise on Wednesday to campaign for his old friend, Abraham Ribicoff, then
Democratic candidate for United States Senator from
Connecticut. As Governor of the Nutmeg State, Ribicoff had been the first Democrat of any prominence
to endorse John Kennedy for President. He had refused the Attorney Generalship when Kennedy was
elected, becoming instead Secretary of Health, Edu-
cation and Welfare. But Abe Ribicoff, after a few
months, had grown restless in the Administration.
When he resigned to run for the Senate, the President
had promised he would do all he could to help insure
Ribicoff's election. Before flying to Connecticut that
morning, the President met, at 9:35, with Bundy and
McCone, who had just returned from the West Coast.

He also found time for second thoughts about
Ambassador Bohlen's departure for Paris. Kenneth
O'Donnell had Bohlen paged at Washington's National Airport, where he was about to board a plane
for New York. "The President wants you to sit in the
meetings," he said. Bohlen reminded O'Donnell that
he was to speak in New York the following day at a
France-Amerique luncheon before embarking on the

liner *United States*. "The President wants you to
break the date," O'Donnell insisted. When Kennedy
took the telephone Bohlen explained the problem: if
he were to cancel the luncheon speech for no apparent reason, all the President's efforts to ensure total
secrecy might be blown sky-high. People would ask
embarrassing questions. Reluctantly, the President
agreed. "Okay," he said, "go ahead."

Before leaving, Bohlen had prepared a handwritten
statement of his own views and recommendations.
He crowded them into a single sheet of yellow paper,
which Dean Rusk read to the Executive Committee
later that day. Although the text has apparently been
lost, Bohlen remembers having written that the
United States was moving into a major crisis with
Russia, and that the missiles must be removed from
Cuba at all costs. While military means of removing
them had to be considered, Bohlen's recommendation
was that diplomatic means should be tried first.

In Connecticut later that day, Kennedy toured
Bridgeport, Waterbury, and New Haven, where some
Yale students booed him while holding up a placard
that read: "More courage, less profile." It was not
Kennedy, the Harvard man, that they were booing.
They were accusing the President of cowardice in
having done nothing to overthrow the Castro regime,
a common Republican complaint of the 1962 campaign. The President answered them lightheartedly:
"I have come back to this center of learning in order
[*applause*] . . . to come back to my college, Yale
[*applause*], and I have enjoyed that warm reception
I've gotten from my fellow Elis as I drove into the
city. But they will learn, as this country has learned,
that the Democratic Party is best for them as it is for
the country."

In Kennedy's absence from Washington, the Executive Committee members sat through much of the day
and into the night in George Ball's conference room at
the State Department. They soon were calling it the

"think tank." The conference room is directly across the corridor from the Under Secretary of State's seventh-floor office. It is a rectangular space, windowless, with leather armchairs marching in straight rows on either side of a long table. The style is Indeterminate Modern, reflecting no man's personal taste. It suggests, instead, the lowest common denominator agreed upon in a committee of warring decorators. People came and went as their departmental duties allowed, some listening, some talking, some scribbling notes. Dean Acheson, sitting in for the first time on that Wednesday, found it all rather formless and confused. When someone was hungry, sandwiches and coffee were sent for. It may have been by tactful design, but, more likely, was a product of the random comings and goings, that Acheson and Adlai Stevenson—who despised each other—never found themselves in the room at the same time, though the record shows that both were there. Acheson, long before the missile crisis, had marked Stevenson down as woolly-minded and soft. Stevenson, for his part, tended to put Acheson in the "warhawk" party when, in private conversations, he allowed himself to criticize Administration foreign policy.

One participant recalls that Dean Rusk—the senior Cabinet officer and, in a sense, the host—refused to exercise the chairman's function, except for a few summarizing remarks after McCone's intelligence briefing. McNamara was deferring to Rusk. Thus, with the President away on the hustings, Robert Kennedy soon emerged as the discussion leader. The President's brother was careful at the beginning not to appear the protagonist of any single course of action. He played the devil's advocate when necessary, asking sharp and—some felt—rude questions. It was his way of forcing one protagonist or another to defend his chosen position. This was brainstorming and some of the older men present did not care to be quizzed by a stripling.

Adlai Stevenson made no secret of his own early distaste, comparing the Attorney General to "a bull in a china shop." Yet he came round at the end to conceding that Robert Kennedy had been the most influential man in the room. Another participant said: "Bobby made Christians of us. We all knew little brother was watching; and keeping a little list of where everyone stood. This had a healthy effect in stimulating real discussion. It inhibited the striking of attitudes. Having him there in the conference room was perhaps better, because it was less inhibiting, than having the President there."

Beginning Tuesday afternoon and thereafter each morning at 8:30, the United States Intelligence Board met to examine the accumulation of U-2 photographs and to estimate the degree of danger. Inevitably a code name had to be invented. This time there were two: PSALM for the intelligence channel, ELITE for the policy channel. The Intelligence Board brought together around one table representatives of the CIA, the Defense Intelligence Agency, the National Security Agency, and the State Department, and intelligence officers of the individual armed services. For the duration of the missiles crisis they met not in Langley, Virginia, at the CIA's enormous headquarters overlooking the George Washington Memorial Highway, but in one of the old red-brick buildings in Foggy Bottom which had been used during the war by the Office of Strategic Services and in its early years by the CIA itself. This put the PSALMists within easy reach of the ELITE meeting at the State Department or in the White House.

That morning, the Intelligence Board produced its first estimate based on the intensified U-2 overflight discoveries. Overnight, out of the scarred earth of San Cristóbal and Guanajay had sprouted mobile launchers. Twenty-eight launch pads appeared to be in various stages of construction and, for the first time, missiles were visible. In PSALM, at least, there was no debate about the meaning of these facts and figures. Two kinds of missiles were going into place: one a 1,000-mile medium-range ballistic missile, a mobile field weapon that could be installed in just a few hours, then shifted elsewhere; the other a 2,200-mile intermediate-range missile, which had to be fired from a fixed position. Both were what the soldiery and the megaton technicians would call "first-strike" weapons, useful in a surprise attack but incapable of surviving a counter-blow. The quick reckoning of the intelligence community was that, with both types operational, the Soviet Union would be able to deliver an initial salvo of something like 40 nuclear warheads on targets in the United States as far west as Wyoming and Montana. This might not be sufficient megatonnage to tilt the strategic balance in Russia's favor, but some felt it might be enough to give Khrushchev powerful new leverage in his dealings with Kennedy. Peering down from an altitude of thirteen miles the U-2 planes could not have been expected to, nor did they, in fact, find any trace of nuclear warheads. But they had managed to capture on film glimpses of unusual buildings with curved roofs. Some of these, as the construction went forward, were to be covered with earth, presumably for cushioning the blast of missiles on lift-off. The intelligence men guessed that these buildings were designed for warhead storage. They agreed that it made no military sense for the Russians to put ballistic missiles into Cuba without also providing nuclear tips.

Acheson recalls that there was considerable dispute within the Executive Committee that Wednesday over the degree of increased danger to the United States from missiles based ninety miles offshore, as against the Soviet ICBMs across the ocean. McNamara stuck to his "a missile is a missile" argument. There was, however, no dispute over the tremendous challenge to American prestige that they represented. Even

Adlai Stevenson, supposedly the soft liner, said: "No politician could have missed the significance of Russian missiles in Cuba. We just had to get them out of there. This was the first time that the Latin Americans were also directly involved or threatened. I felt this was extremely important. They were one with us. They could not consider this a remote quarrel between the United States and Russia, as some perhaps were tempted to do earlier."

The overhanging question, still unanswered, was how to get the missiles out of Cuba without war. In the course of that day's discussion, six alternatives, or separate tracks, were reviewed.

Track A called for doing nothing immediately. Andrei Gromyko, the Soviet Foreign Minister, had an appointment to see the President on the following day. Some sentiment developed for having the President confront Gromyko with the photographic evidence; then demand that the Soviet Union remove its missiles from Cuba. This was rejected. The majority felt that it would be a mistake to give the Russians advance warning so long as armed action remained an open possibility.

Track B was to send an emissary to Khrushchev, tell him privately that the United States knew the missiles were there, and insist that he remove them. The hazard of this course, quickly perceived, was that Khrushchev might seize the diplomatic initiative, mobilizing certain of the nonaligned countries and left-wing opinion in the West to push the United States toward a conference no less disastrous than Munich, in which the President would find himself under the heaviest kind of pressure to trade off NATO bases in Europe for Russian missile bases in Cuba.

Track C, arraigning the Soviet Union and Cuba before the United Nations Security Council, held little promise for two reasons: the Russian veto and the fact that Valerian Zorin of the Soviet Union happened to be chairman of the Council for October.

Each of these alternatives met the specifications of the diplomatic approach favored initially by McGeorge Bundy and Stevenson. In addition there was some talk of sending an emissary to Castro. Thomas C. Mann, then United States Ambassador to Mexico, happened to be in Washington that week. He was asked to stand by, though he was not told of the proposed secret mission to Havana. Mann did not, in fact, learn about the crisis until the following Sunday, after he had returned to Mexico. Another suggestion, also discarded, was to treat the whole thing as a regrettable mistake which the Soviet Union should be asked to put right, without a great public uproar. This recalled Khrushchev's willingness to treat the first U-2 incident on May 1, 1960—when Francis Gary Powers was shot down over Soviet territory—as a blunder committed by subordinate officials without the knowledge or approval of President Eisenhower. The remaining three tracks called for military action, in one degree or another. It was on these three that the discussion finally centered.

Track D was an embargo on all military shipments to Cuba, to be enforced by a naval blockade. It came to be known within the Executive Committee as "the slow track." This meant confronting the Russians directly, not Fidel Castro, because it was Russian ships (or foreign ships under Soviet charter) that were carrying military supplies to Castro across the wide Atlantic. The embargo had several advantages: it could be graduated in severity to exclude offensive weapons alone, or all armaments, or all strategic goods including petroleum; it meant an exercise of American sea power in waters already controlled by the United States Navy; moreover, it was less provocative, consequently less dangerous, than a direct attack on Cuba by air or sea. On the negative side, a blockade might be repugnant to Britain and other maritime nations of the Western alliance which traded with Cuba and were highly

sensitive to any apparent infringement of the free-
dom-of-the-seas principle. Moreover, it was common-
ly regarded as an act of war. Vice President Johnson
—no lawyer himself—had said as much just a few
days earlier in denouncing Senator Keating's demand
for a Cuban embargo. Although some regretted the
Vice President's pronouncement, verbal consistency
seemed far less important to the men assembled in
George Ball's conference room than finding the right
lever that could dislodge the missiles from Cuba.

Track E called for a surprise attack to eliminate
the missile installations by pinpoint bombing. This
came to be known as the "fast track." It meant using
jet bombers with the precision of a highly skilled
surgeon, who cuts away diseased tissue, leaving the
healthy tissue intact. The chief argument of the "fast
track" proponents was that the evidence so far uncov-
ered left no room for doubt that the Russians were
building a major strategic base in the Caribbean, designed not so much to defend Castro as to intimidate
the United States. They estimated that at least 16,
perhaps 32, missiles would be ready for firing within
one week. A surprise attack would, of course, kill
Russians manning the missile sites in addition to
some Cubans living near by. This would put Khrushchev under strong pressure to retaliate—against the
United States if his missiles were ready, perhaps
elsewhere if they were not—apart from raising a great
outcry of protest against the President as a murderous bully. There was the added danger, bombers
being rather less precise than surgeon's knives, that
not all the missile bases would in fact be eliminated,
perhaps provoking a Soviet officer to fire the surviving missiles and obliterate an American city.

Track F, not seriously considered that day because
it would take too long to mount, was an invasion of
Cuba. The Pentagon had kept its contingency plans
up to date, ever since the fiasco at the Bay of Pigs.
But a military assault of sufficient power to capture

the island, subdue the Russian troops stationed there
and overthrow the Castro dictatorship, would demand preparations that could hardly be concealed for
more than a few hours. For all these reasons, Track F
was put aside, to be re-examined later.

George Ball was the first to argue vigorously
against the air strike idea. He felt it was an irreversible step. Every nation ought to act in accordance
with its own traditions, Ball argued. If the United
States were to launch a surprise attack it would be
violating its own best traditions and doing itself ir-
reparable harm, regardless of the military outcome.
To the surprise of many in the room, Robert Kennedy picked up Ball's argument. Recalling Pearl Harbor, he said passionately: "My brother is not going to
be the Tojo of the 1960's." Moreover, the Attorney
General doubted that a surprise air strike, by itself,
would take out all the missiles. An invasion would
have to follow, taking a horrendous toll of innocent
Cuban lives.* A decent regard for humanity ought
to rule out any surprise attack, he said.

The challenge to Robert Kennedy—at thirty-seven
years old already the Attorney General and to all in-
tents assistant President—in his new role as moralist
of the Administration came from a man old enough to
be his father. Dean Acheson, sixty-nine, former Secretary of State, chief architect of the Truman Administration's cold war policies, disagreed sharply.
He rejected the Pearl Harbor analogy with majestic
scorn. For more than a century the Monroe Doctrine

---

* On October 13, 1964, in a campaign speech at Rockville
Centre, New York, Robert Kennedy said the President's intelligence advisers had estimated that 25,000 Cubans would
be killed if the decision were made to bomb the missile sites
and the air bases in Cuba. "We could have gone in and
knocked out all their bases—there wasn't any question about
it—and then started bargaining," Kennedy said. But the
President would have no part of a "Pearl Harbor in re-
verse," because of "his belief in what is right and what is
wrong."

had made clear to all the world that the United States would not tolerate the intrusion of any European power into the Americas, Acheson said. Now that it had happened, the intrusion could only be regarded as a definitely unfriendly act. Both the President and the Congress had warned in unmistakable terms that the United States would be forced to act if the Soviet Union installed offensive weapons in Cuba. He cited the Presidential warnings on September 4 and 13 and the Congressional resolution of October 3, authorizing the President to prevent "by whatever means may be necessary, including the use of arms," the creation in Cuba of a foreign military base endangering the security of the United States. Surely that was warning enough, Acheson said. The question of surprise attack simply did not arise.

The duel between Robert Kennedy and Dean Acheson was not settled that day. It was, in any case, to be the President's decision. And before he could determine his own course of action, a great deal of staff work remained to be done. The Pentagon had to calculate what kinds of military units, what numbers of men, and what quantities of equipment would be required for either the air strike or the invasion alternatives, quite apart from the demands of a Caribbean blockade. The State Department started to explore the prospects of enlisting support from Latin America and the European allies, many of whom had lived for years in the shadow of Soviet missiles and were inclined to consider Cuba a peculiar American obsession. There was, finally, the need to keep overflying the missile sites several times each day, developing and analyzing miles of film, frame by frame. Hour by hour, round the clock, the launch pads were being rushed to completion. Everyone in the room recognized that once they were operational the danger would take on a new dimension.

That Wednesday, Major General Sir Kenneth William Dobson Strong, who had been Dwight Eisenhower's intelligence chief in North Africa, Sicily, Italy, France, and Germany, visited the Pentagon on official business. General Strong, now Director of the Joint Intelligence Bureau in the British Defense Ministry, was in Washington attending a conference "on intelligence methodology" with his counterparts from Canada, Australia and New Zealand, as a guest of the American intelligence chiefs. Although his American friends were careful not to talk about the hidden crisis, General Strong noticed beds being carried into the Pentagon offices of certain high officials. He put this together with the oddly preoccupied manner of the American participants at conference sessions. Some arrived late and left early; others were called to the telephone during the conference and never seemed to return. It did not require the talents of an old professional like General Strong to divine that something big was happening. He decided to alert the British Ambassador, David Ormsby Gore.

President Kennedy returned late that night from Connecticut. The Attorney General and Ted Sorensen were at the airport to meet and to brief him on the day's deliberations. He heard them out and went to his bedroom, well aware that whatever the Executive Committee might recommend, he alone would have to decide in just a few hours whether it was to be peace or war.

*This is the week when I had better earn my
salary.*
—JOHN F. KENNEDY to Dean Acheson, October
18, 1962

THAT THURSDAY, the President invited Dean Acheson to the White House. The tall, elegant, sharp-
tongued former Secretary of State found Kennedy sitting alone in his study. They talked about forty-five
minutes, considering the choices open to the President—blockade versus air strike. Kennedy had been
fully briefed on Wednesday's discussion in the Executive Committee. He mentioned the Cuba-Pearl Harbor analogy, which Acheson had scorned when Robert Kennedy raised it the previous day. The President
reviewed the bidding. Either way it would be a painful decision. Acheson looked ahead beyond the Presidential decision, to the day when the Allies and the
world at large would have to be informed. "Talking
to de Gaulle," he said, "will be a problem. We have
no ambassador in Paris. Chip Bohlen will be at sea
for several days. It's not the kind of thing that should
be left to a chargé d'affaires." Acheson suggested sending Vice President Johnson to Paris. Letting the suggestion drop, Kennedy got up from his rocking chair
and gazed out the French windows for a long time in
silence.

"This is the week," the President said at last, "when
I had better earn my salary."

Acheson reflected gratefully that Kennedy, not he, carried the burden of decision.

The Executive Committee was to meet twice with the President that day, at 11 A.M. and again at 10 P.M. At five o'clock he would be receiving Gromyko. The newspapers Thursday morning carried a report that the Defense Department had started a build-up of American air power in the Southeastern states, nearest to Cuba. It happened to be true. Somewhat defensively, the Pentagon confirmed the deployment of certain air units to the Southeast, calling it "an ordinary thing to do" in the light of the fact that Castro now possessed modern MIG jet fighters. There was no mention of missiles. To maintain the outward appearance that all was well, the President at 9:30 that morning handed out various aviation trophies. At ten o'clock he held a routine Cabinet meeting on various domestic matters. Kennedy did not once mention Cuba to his Cabinet. Those Cabinet officers who were privy to the unseen crisis—Rusk, McNamara, Dillon, and Robert Kennedy—had little to say to their colleagues. The Attorney General looked around for Edward R. Murrow, director of the United States Information Agency. He found instead Murrow's deputy, Donald Wilson.

"Where is Ed?" he inquired.

"He is ill at home in Pawling [New York]," Wilson replied.

"Will he be back in a few days?"

"Not a chance."

The Attorney General looked vaguely troubled. "You'd better keep in touch," he said. Wilson had been planning to visit his mother in New Jersey that week end. "I think you'd better stick around over the week end," Robert Kennedy said. "We may need you." Although Don Wilson was an old friend and touch-football teammate of the Kennedy brothers, Bobby told him nothing that day.

In Rusk's conference room at the State Department

that morning, the discussion had to do chiefly with
tactics: whether the President should tell the world
about the missiles in Cuba before acting to remove
them. Dean Rusk had been careful not to identify
himself with one school or the other—hawks or doves,
as they later came to be known. He felt it was important to reserve his own position. When the final
recommendation was ready he would have to urge it
on the President, whichever way the decision went.
That morning, however, Rusk spoke out against a surprise attack. Quite apart from the risk of provoking
a spasm reaction in the Kremlin, he felt it would be
costly in terms of political support. If the President
acted without first consulting the Organization of
American States, or the United Nations, or without
any prior effort to approach the Russians, he would
forfeit support round the world. It later developed
that the Secretary of State was not so much recommending prior consultation as thinking aloud. In the
afternoon session he seemed to turn the proposition
around. Starting from the assumption that the United
States could not tolerate the continued presence of
Russian missiles in Cuba, he suggested Tuesday, October 23, as the deadline. If by that date the missile
sites were still under construction, the United States
should then inform its chief allies—he mentioned
Britain, France, West Germany, Italy and Turkey—
that it would use force to remove them. About
Wednesday, October 24, the United States Air Force
would strike the missile bases, the attack to be simultaneous with a public statement and a message to
Khrushchev, warning him in plain language that Soviet counteraction would mean war. Taking the missiles out would not be the end of the matter, Rusk
predicted. "If we don't do this," he said, "we go down
with a whimper. Maybe it's better to go down with
a bang."

Rusk's apparent turnabout illustrates the futility of
trying to sort out the hawks from the doves. The

fact is that nearly every man in the room changed his
position at least once—and some more than once—
during that anxious week of brainstorming. Rusk's
two-part soliloquy—as he saw it—had nothing to do
with advocating one course or the other; his purpose
was to state each proposition as persuasively as he
could in order that both might then be critically
examined and debated. This left him open to the
charge of straddling. Other participants called his
views "opaque." In a *Saturday Evening Post* article,
published after the crisis, Stewart Alsop and Charles
Bartlett wrote: "Secretary Rusk's position does not
come through loud and clear—he appears to have
been a dawk or a hove from the start." As for Mc-
George Bundy, treated far more gently by the same
authors, other Executive Committee members agree
that he changed position twice. Bundy started out
talking of a diplomatic approach, next argued for
doing nothing, and then became an airstrike advocate.

All this retrospective pigeonholing loses sight of
the essential point. The President alone, as Commander in Chief, had the power to decide and did in fact
give the orders. The President's was the controlling
intelligence. He ran the operation, one official recalls, "like a lieutenant runs a platoon in combat."
Bundy, Rusk, Stevenson, and the rest were there to
advise him. He listened, then made his own decisions.

Each meeting opened with McCone's intelligence
briefing. There was no agenda, only a checklist of
topics which Bundy would have typed up a few minutes beforehand. The President would then call, in
turn, on Rusk and McNamara, leading to a general
discussion. Kennedy did a lot of listening. He was
careful to give each of the secondary figures—Gilpatric, Nitze or Ball—his opportunity to be heard. When
the time came he would state his own conclusion,
often understating it. There were no scenes of high
drama. Sometimes he would signal his decision by a
nod of the head. Bundy would then distill the essence

of the discussion in the form of a National Security Action Memorandum (NSAM), showing where the matter stood. At all times the President was in control of himself. Those who knew him best could sense that he was impatient or irritated when, on occasion, he would tap his front teeth with his forefinger. Long after the meeting had adjourned, back in the White House living quarters, the President would work off his tensions in solitude. Sitting in his rocker with a yellow legal-sized pad in his lap, he would cover page after page with notes of all kinds in that quirky scrawl of his, littering the floor with sheets of paper. Then the President's secretary, Mrs. Evelyn Lincoln, would scoop them up. One of the few who could decipher Kennedy's penmanship, Mrs. Lincoln would edit the notes, then type them neatly for his use the following day.

At the morning session with the President on Thursday, the Intelligence Board reported that the first Soviet medium-range missile in Cuba could be ready for launching in eighteen hours. The Joint Chiefs of Staff had started ordering precautionary troop movements. It began to appear that the decision-making machinery was racing the clock. There were now two elements of urgency: first, the danger that more missiles would soon be operational; second, the possibility that in spite of all the elaborate security measures, a leak might alert the Kremlin to the preparations under way in Washington. It was at least conceivable that if Khrushchev discovered what was going on, he would seize the initiative by serving an ultimatum before Kennedy was ready to serve his own.

There was talk that morning of ultimate policy goals. Should the President limit his objective to the simple removal of Soviet missiles, or use the occasion to get rid of Castro at the same time? The first alternative could perhaps be accomplished by the naval blockade. The second certainly would demand a full-scale invasion.

The President listened more than he spoke. Though, when he put questions, the others felt they could discern his trend of thought. For Kennedy the talk of invading Cuba inevitably called up memories of the Bay of Pigs, his most humiliating failure. It was clear to everyone in the room that there must never be another such disaster.

Then came the turn of the lawyers present—Ball and Acheson most prominent among them—to consider the legality of each alternative. Acheson took the position that legal niceties were so much pompous foolishness in a situation where the essential security of the United States, its prestige, its pledged word to defend the Americas, was threatened. Although Fidel Castro had recently declared himself a Marxist-Leninist, Cuba did not belong to the Warsaw Pact. Thus an attack on Cuba would not necessarily bring the Soviet Union into a state of war with the United States, whereas an attack on Poland, for example, most assuredly would. Ball argued that a naval blockade, though traditionally regarded as an act of war, would have more "color of legality." Abram J. Chayes, Legal Adviser to the Secretary of State, was away in Paris for a series of meetings aimed at persuading the Western Allies to stop trading with Cuba. In his absence, Chayes' deputy, Leonard C. Meeker, presented a legal analysis suggesting, for the first time, that the blockade might better be called a defensive quarantine. He borrowed the phrase, with due acknowledgement, from Franklin D. Roosevelt's "quarantine-the-aggressor" speech. By noon, as Kennedy left to receive the Japanese Finance Minister, Eifaku Sato, it began to appear that the blockade advocates might prevail. Legalities had less to do with this than the practical argument that a naval blockade would avoid killing Russians and give the Kremlin time to reflect.

At 2:30 P.M. the discussion was resumed at the State Department, without the President. His absence was anything but accidental. Robert Kennedy frequently urged his brother to stay away. "I felt there was less true give-and-take with the President in the room," he recalls. "There was the danger that, by indicating his own views or leanings, he would cause the others just to fall into line. I felt the process of discussion, of truly hammering out the alternatives, was essential. Though there were some who didn't receive it with great enthusiasm."

Sir David Ormsby Gore, now Lord Harlech, received two official visitors that Thursday in the British Embassy. Although the Ambassador enjoyed an extraordinary intimacy with the President, going back to the days when young Jack Kennedy had lived in London as the second son of Joseph P. Kennedy, the American Ambassador to the Court of St. James's, he was still unaware of the threatening crisis. His visitors—Major General Sir Kenneth Strong and Sir Hugh Stephenson, then Deputy Under Secretary of State at the Foreign Office—had an intriguing story to tell. There was the matter of certain beds General Strong had observed being trundled into certain Pentagon offices. Also the curious behavior of their American hosts, who kept disappearing from joint meetings on intelligence methods or failing to show up at their own parties for the Commonwealth visitors. What did it mean? Clearly "something funny" was going on, something the Americans, for reasons best known to themselves, did not want to tell the British about. Putting their heads together, the three knights decided it had to be a major international crisis, probably a Cuban crisis. They agreed to meet again the following day in order to examine the mystery more closely.

At 4:30 P.M., Dean Rusk and Llewellyn Thompson went to the White House to brief the President in advance of his meeting with Gromyko, who arrived at five o'clock sharp. The Soviet Foreign Minister settled into a stuffed chair facing Kennedy's rocker and picked up where Khrushchev had left off in his talk two days earlier with Ambassador Kohler. He assured the President that the Soviet Union would do nothing about Berlin until after the American elections, November 6, unless the West were to force Moscow's hand. After the elections there would have to be some dialogue over Berlin, leading to concrete results. These Gromyko defined as a German peace treaty and the "normalization" of Berlin's situation, meaning the establishment of a "free city" and the withdrawal of Western garrisons. If there was no agreement, the Soviet Government would be "compelled"—he stressed the word "compelled" by repeating it—to sign a separate peace with East Germany and take all necessary steps in pursuance of that action. Threats by the Western powers would have no effect. Knowing the President enjoyed frank talk, Gromyko wanted to be no less frank than Khrushchev at Vienna. No one took Berlin seriously as a NATO base, hence nothing would be lost in removing the city from NATO's protection.

Kennedy replied that while the United States was always ready to talk about Berlin, the continued presence of Western troops was vital to the survival of the city and its freedom. If they were withdrawn, the city would fall under East German control and other American commitments round the world might be questioned. Gromyko dismissed the President's objections, saying the Soviet Union was prepared to offer solemn guarantees that Berlin's freedom would be respected. He then obliquely raised the question of a Kennedy-Khrushchev conference before the end of the year. The President said he was ready to talk with Khrushchev; though not about Berlin, because other friendly nations had an equal interest in the city's future. If there was to be such a meeting it could have no fixed agenda. At this point the talk turned to Cuba.

Gromyko complained of what he called the anti-Cuba campaign in the United States, particularly of attacks on shipping by Cuban exile groups. All this could lead to great misfortune, he said. Cuba, after all, belonged to the Cubans, not to the United States. How, in any case, could little Cuba (a baby, he called it) hurt or threaten the giant United States? If he might once again be frank, knowing the President appreciated frankness, 1962 was not 1812. In the age of modern weaponry, the President's authority to call up 150,000 reservists had no significance. He was under instructions to make it clear that the Soviet Union gave assistance to Cuba for the sole purpose of strengthening Cuba's capacity to defend herself and to develop her agriculture. The training of Cuban soldiers by Soviet specialists was by no means an offensive measure. If it were otherwise, the Soviet Government would never have involved itself in such assistance. Hence, in the name of the Soviet Government and of Chairman Khrushchev himself, he was appealing to President Kennedy not to allow any actions with respect to Cuba that would be incompatible with peace and with the United Nations Charter.

President Kennedy replied that the United States had no intention of invading Cuba. But, beginning in July, the Soviet Union had started an arms build-up there. As there was no invasion threat Kennedy found it hard to understand this change of Soviet policy. Moreover, the arms shipments to Cuba had profoundly affected American opinion, as Ambassador Dobrynin could testify. The President said he had tried to calm the reaction, but the Russians ought to understand that their activities in Cuba were extremely serious; and they had given no satisfactory explanation.

Gromyko protested that there had already been one invasion attempt and it was well known how this had turned out. The President cut him short, saying he had discussed this with Khrushchev at their Vienna meeting in June 1961, admitting then that the Bay of Pigs had been a mistake.

The President gave Gromyko a clear opportunity to set the record straight by referring back to the repeated assurances of Khrushchev and Dobrynin that the missiles in Cuba were nothing but antiaircraft weapons incapable of striking targets in the United States. He pointed his meaning by reading aloud a portion of his September 4 statement that the United States would not tolerate the establishment of a Soviet strategic base in Cuba. The President also cited his own assurances to the American people that Soviet military assistance programs were purely defensive, and his warning that any change in that estimate would have the gravest consequences. Gromyko stubbornly repeated the old assurances, which the President now knew to be lies. Kennedy did not confront him with the facts. If Gromyko knew the truth about the full extent of the Soviet commitment in Cuba, he gave the President no sign during the two hours and fifteen minutes they spent together.

Leaving the White House that Thursday evening in a mood of unwonted joviality, the Soviet Foreign Minister described his talk with the President as "useful, very useful."

When Gromyko left to dress for dinner at the State Department, the President turned to Rusk and Thompson with a question: perhaps it was a mistake not to have told Gromyko that the Americans knew the truth about those missiles in Cuba? (This was a point raised afterward by some critics of American policy, who wondered why the President had not confronted Gromyko with the evidence—and thus offered the Russians a last chance to draw back.) Both Rusk and Thompson assured Kennedy that he had done the right thing. They pointed out that until the President had determined what steps he would take to dislodge the

missiles, premature disclosure would have given the
Russians a tactical advantage.*

With the hour of decision fast approaching, Ken-
nedy had called on a man he greatly admired—
Robert A. Lovett, once Harry Truman's Secretary of
Defense—to provide a fresh judgment. While the
President fenced with Gromyko, Bundy briefed
Lovett on the details and then led him upstairs to
see Kennedy. Lovett was to join the Executive Com-
mittee for its climactic sessions just ahead. Apart from
Acheson and McCloy, he was the only private citi-
zen to be called in by the President.

The same day, Kennedy also notified former Presidents Truman and Eisenhower. John McCone, a California Republican, volunteered to tell Eisenhower. Although McCone has refused to divulge what passed
between them at Gettysburg, there is reason to believe that Eisenhower took a skeptical view, suspect-
ing perhaps that Kennedy might be playing politics
with Cuba on the eve of Congressional elections. Mc-
Cone enjoyed Eisenhower's confidence, having served
in his Administration as chairman of the Atomic
Energy Commission. But Ike evidently found it hard
to forget or forgive Kennedy's dismissal of the
speeches by Senator Keating, warning of the Soviet
arms build-up.

Rusk's dinner for Gromyko at eight o'clock that
night added nothing to the Administration's understanding of Soviet actions or motives. The two became embroiled in a long colloquy over Berlin and
whether it was the Russians or the Americans who
had started the cold war. The dinner did, however,
produce a comic by-product when McNamara and
McCone strode into the State Department lobby just
as Gromyko had gone up to the eighth floor dining

---

* McGeorge Bundy recalls: "It made all the difference—I
felt then and have felt since—that the Russians were caught
pretending, in a clumsy way, that they had not done what it
was clear to the whole world they had in fact done."

room. Reporters and cameramen, out in force to record Gromyko's arrival, wrongly assumed that the Secretary of Defense and the CIA chief were going to the dinner. To make certain, one reporter asked if that was their destination. He accepted McNamara's "Yes" at face value. In fact they were on their way to the "think tank" in George Ball's conference room one floor below. A more cynical reporter might have boggled at the notion of McCone's breaking bread with Gromyko. This one did not. There were other narrow scrapes that day as the Administration nervously clutched its secrets. One sharp-eyed middle-level official said to his boss: "I know there is something going on that you don't want to talk about. But if security is all that tight, maybe you'd better tell all those big wheels from across the river to get their cars off the street." The boss looked out the window, saw for himself that the diplomatic entrance was jammed with long black official limousines bearing easily identified license plates. Thereafter, all but one of the limousines disappeared into the basement garage.

That evening in Ball's conference room—while Rusk and Gromyko were refighting the cold-war battles of the Forties and Fifties a floor above them—the Executive Committee members found a consensus developing against an air strike. They had divided into two groups, George Ball heading the blockade team, and McGeorge Bundy the air-strike team. They had been split almost evenly at the start: McCone, Dillon, Taylor, Acheson, Nitze, and eventually Bundy on the side of using American air power to "take out" the Russian missile sites; McNamara, Gilpatric, Robert Kennedy, Thompson, Ball, and now also Lovett for a naval blockade. (Adlai Stevenson had returned to New York for the conclusion of the general debate in the United Nations General Assembly.) Each team put its case as forcefully as it could in an exercise of comparative persuasiveness, similar to the war

games played at military schools. At one stage the
air-strike team suggested asking the Swiss Government, which looks after American interests in Cuba,
to warn Castro in advance of the projected air attack, parallel with a warning to the Russians that
they should evacuate their people from the missile
sites. Tommy Thompson dealt with that suggestion.
He argued that not much was to be gained by dealing
with Castro, through the Swiss or otherwise. It was
the Russians who had put missiles into Cuba. This
was a major departure from Soviet policy and must
have been fully considered in the Kremlin. Hence
the Russians alone could take them out.

The air-strike team countered with the argument
that a naval blockade could prove more dangerous
than an air attack. The Russians, for example, might
retaliate for the sinking of one of their ships by calling on their submarines in the area to sink an American ship. Then, inescapably, it would be up the ladder of escalating war, rung by rung.

Dean Rusk's impression was that, after hearing the
pros and cons, the protagonists on both sides persuaded themselves that either course was difficult, far
more difficult than they had imagined before examining the pitfalls and complexities. The overriding consideration was the President's own belief that an air
strike by itself would accomplish little and would inevitably have to be followed by an invasion of Cuba.
Ambassador Thompson had reinforced the President's
own caution, arguing that, of all possible courses, a
surprise attack on the missile sites was by far the
most hazardous. It meant killing Russians, and
Khrushchev, he warned, was notoriously impulsive.

That evening, Douglas Dillon changed his position.
"I had wanted an air strike," he recalls. "I had assumed the Russians would deceive us. I expected
nothing else. Nor did I believe that the Russians
would necessarily send their missiles against the
United States if we attacked their Cuban bases. What

changed my mind was Bobby Kennedy's argument that we ought to be true to ourselves as Americans, that surprise attack was not in our tradition. Frankly, these considerations had not occurred to me until Bobby raised them so eloquently."

There is general agreement that McNamara helped the Attorney General mightily with his now-celebrated argument on "maintaining the options." He contended the decision confronting the President was not of the either-or variety. Let blockade be his first option, the contraband list limited at the start to offensive weapons. If that failed, the President would then have a choice of responses. He could decide to deny the Cubans other kinds of cargo—petroleum, for example—or he could move up the scale to an air strike, or even, at the far end, to an invasion. If one form of pressure failed in its purpose, then another, more severe, pressure could be applied. Nothing would be lost by starting from the bottom of the scale. Bundy credits Dillon with the refinement that brought about his own conversion. The Secretary of the Treasury's clinching argument in favour of the blockade was that it could be applied without losing the option to launch an air strike later. If, however, the air strike was to be the first step, other options would be closed.

At ten o'clock, the exhausted committee members were asked to rejoin the President. Nine of them piled into a single limousine to avoid attracting attention by the sudden arrival of a whole cavalcade at that late hour. Edwin Martin chose to walk the ten blocks to the White House. In the crush of bodies, someone remarked: "What if we get into a collision?"

The meeting with the President, which ran on past midnight, confirmed the trend toward a naval blockade. Kennedy promptly assigned Sorensen to start drafting the speech in which he would disclose the presence of Soviet missiles in Cuba and proclaim measures for their removal. Roswell Gilpatric handed

General Taylor a batch of assignments for the Pentagon planners. He asked the Chairman of the Joint
Chiefs to supply: 1) a list of riot-control equipment
that the United States could provide to Latin-American governments should any of them need help in
maintaining internal security; 2) a list of offensive
weapons to be barred from Cuba by the blockade;
3) a study showing which of the Latin American
countries could assist in blockading Cuba; 4) another
study, citing the pros and cons of extending the
blockade to cover airplanes bound for Cuba, as well
as ships at sea; 5) a report on the ramifications of
working with Alpha 66 and other Cuban exile groups.

That night, Robert Kennedy telephoned his deputy,
Katzenbach, at home and asked him to get started
on a brief establishing the legal basis for a blockade
of Cuba. George Ball's assistant, George Springsteen,
called Abram Chayes away from his shipping discussions in Paris. It was a conversation remarkable for
its brevity and for what was left unsaid.

"Come on home," Springsteen said to the State Department's Legal Adviser.

"What do you mean? What's going on? Is it important?"

"Sure, it's important. Come on home."

"What is it, Cuba?"

"Just shut up and come on home."

Abe Chayes came on home.

*The President may have to develop a cold to-
morrow.*
—KENNETH O'DONNELL to Pierre Salinger in
Chicago, October 19, 1962

PRESIDENT KENNEDY left Washington Friday morning for one more round of campaign speeches, still
faithfully keeping his engagements in order to avoid
giving alarm. He was fretful and discouraged when
he stepped into the plane for Cleveland. The Joint
Chiefs of Staff had delayed his departure a half hour
to plead for an air strike or an invasion, anything
but the naval blockade that the President's advisers
had agreed Thursday night was the least dangerous
first step. Acheson was still adamant in opposing the
blockade. Dean Rusk kept raising second thoughts.
McGeorge Bundy was torn at having to choose between two courses of action that seemed to him
equally bleak. The war council was to resume its
discussions at ten o'clock in George Ball's conference
room with the outcome again in doubt. The President broke away, leaving word that his brother Robert was to call him back from the hustings as soon
as he was needed in Washington.

That morning, Pierre Salinger had confronted the
President in his bedroom, still half-dressed, with the
unwelcome news that certain reporters were asking
questions about troop movements in the direction of
Florida. What could he tell them? The President instructed Salinger to say that there was "nothing to"
such reports. The portly press secretary was not

himself persuaded. But, having been told nothing more, he passed the word to inquiring reporters. The Pentagon, fending off queries later in the day about a published report by Paul Scott and Robert S. Allen about missiles in Cuba, took the occasion to issue a two-in-one denial. It said the Government had "no information indicating the presence of offensive weapons in Cuba," adding that no alert had been ordered or "any emergency measures" set in motion against Cuba. The alert, in fact, had just been ordered. Messages went out at 1:20 P.M. on Friday to the Atlantic and Caribbean commands, warning of possible air attacks on the Panama Canal, Ramey Air Force Base, and the Naval Station at Roosevelt Roads, Puerto Rico. Hawk antiaircraft missile batteries were directed to increase their readiness for possible action. Somehow the President's secret remained a secret; the Pentagon's deliberate double lie probably helped. But throughout the day suspicion kept rising, notably when official word came that Defense Secretary McNamara had instructed the Joint Chiefs not to leave Washington for a six-week period so they could consult on "budget planning." Rusk started more reporters guessing when he canceled a speech before the Business Council at Hot Springs pleading "press of business." (The speech was delivered instead by William C. Foster, head of the Arms Control and Disarmament Agency.) The United States Chamber of Commerce, meeting in Washington the same day, had invited George Ball to speak. Ball went through with it, knowing that he would be asked sharp questions about Cuba and that he would have to dodge them. He felt it was important to maintain some semblance of the business-as-usual façade.

For the British, at least, the secret was fast losing its mystery. That morning Ambassador Ormsby Gore called in Sir Kenneth Strong and Sir Hugh Stephenson, the two visiting Whitehall officials who had sensed that a crisis of some sort was brewing. They sat round the circular table in the Ambassador's office and speculated together. The evidence of the President's repeated public warnings against any Russian move to install offensive weapons in Cuba persuaded them that Soviet missiles had probably been discovered there. With the receipt of Ormsby Gore's cable, the British Government became the first to know of the impending crisis; though, like other Allied governments, it had neither been informed nor consulted.

That Friday, with Ed Murrow still ailing, Don Wilson was called to the State Department, briefed on the bare facts of the crisis ahead by George Ball and Ed Martin, and told of the United States Information Agency's crisis assignment. His first task was to make certain that the President's speech announcing the blockade would be heard as widely as possible in Cuba. He was warned to tell no one. Wilson went back to his office on Pennsylvania Avenue, pondered the problem and decided the only feasible way of getting a mass audience in Cuba for the President's speech was to supplement the Voice of America's short-wave transmissions with standard broadcasts in Spanish through privately owned radio stations in the Southeastern states. This meant putting together quietly a network of stations in just a few hours. Wilson's problem was how to approach the station managers, asking that they abandon their own commercial programming in English and broadcast the Voice of America's Spanish-language transmissions instead, without explaining what had happened in Cuba and what the President proposed to do about it. After consulting Rusk and Bundy, Wilson put a strange request to the Bell Telephone representative at the White House, whose usual concern was to make sure that correspondents covering the President had enough lines to get their stories out wherever he and they happened to be—at an airport, a railroad siding, or a crowded convention hall. Wilson asked the telephone company representative to clear lines to all the stations that would make up his proposed Spanish-language network without letting the stations know.

While the President campaigned in Cleveland, stopping in Springfield, Illinois, to deposit a wreath at Abraham Lincoln's tomb on his way to Chicago, the Executive Committee met all day long at the State Department. The doubts about either course—blockade or air strike—were heard all over again, the familiar arguments rehearsed. Bundy prepared a written statement summarizing the air-strike argument; Alexis Johnson, with Paul Nitze's assistance, drafted what came to be called the blockade scenario. The object of the naval blockade, they wrote, was not to bring down Fidel Castro but to remove the Soviet threat to the hemisphere. It would be limited to offensive weapons, not interfering with other cargoes. They rated the probability of Khrushchev's acceptance as "high but not certain." If the Russians refused, however, their likely response could be a blockade of Berlin. All hands joined in the war game of riposte and counterriposte. Every conceivable unpleasant consequence was examined. What, for example, if the President should order an air strike? Then suppose that the Russians—recognizing their tactical disadvantage in a Caribbean confrontation where American sea and air power was paramount —should respond by striking the Jupiter missile sites in Turkey or moving against Iran, both countries on their own frontier where Soviet power was paramount. Surely this was a more accurate parallel than Cuba-Berlin? "Could be," Tommy Thompson muttered gloomily. "The Russians like parallel situations." With Bohlen on his way to France that morning, Thompson had swiftly won the admiration and respect of the President and the others by his astonishing readiness to produce at any hour of the day or night a shrewd guess as to Khrushchev's likely response. It was Thompson who made the point that the Russians were impressed by legalities, even though they had a maddening way of twisting legal interpretations to justify every ferocity they had inflicted on their own people and the rest of the world. If, for example, the Organization of American States should pass a resolution endorsing the blockade, Moscow might be inclined to take it seriously. This would require a two-thirds majority of the twenty voting American Republics—at least fourteen affirmatives votes—and there was no assurance the votes would be forthcoming.

Katzenbach for the Justice Department and Meeker for the Legal Adviser's Office agreed that an OAS resolution, if it could be passed, would provide solid legal support for the blockade. Even if the President were forced to act without OAS sanction, Katzenbach felt, it should be possible to establish a legal basis. Meeker was less certain. There was talk also of Constitutional questions. Should the President summon Congress back to Washington, and ask for a declaration of war? This was quickly discarded. As Commander in Chief, Kennedy had ample inherent powers to impose a blockade, acting in defense of the national interest against the clear and present danger of hostile missiles ninety miles offshore. Acheson, the international lawyer, contended this was no time to worry about legal formalities. The nation's security was at stake. The world would understand that the President had done no more and no less than the situation required. If he failed to order an armed strike against the missile bases, he would be imperiling the security of the United States and the whole of the free world.

Again Robert Kennedy challenged Acheson, not on legal but humane grounds. Returning to the Pearl Harbor-in-reverse argument, the Attorney General said his brother simply could not order an air strike.

A great deal more was at stake than the Soviet missiles in Cuba and the threat they represented. The ideals and convictions of the American people made such an attack repugnant. For the United States to attack a small country like Cuba without warning, he argued, would damage beyond repair both America's standing in the world and its own conscience. Vice President Lyndon Johnson, who less than two weeks earlier had chided the Republicans for advocating a blockade ("Stopping a Russian ship is an act of war," he had said on October 6), sat silent through this exchange. Maxwell Taylor, seemingly impressed by the speech of Robert Kennedy, agreed that a surprise attack was out of the question. "Max is a moral man," one participant recalls. "He showed what a moral man he is by recommending that we give the Cubans twenty-four hours' advance notice—and then strike the missile bases."

The air-strike champions were losing ground and by nightfall they knew it. Dean Acheson decided he had come to the end of his usefulness. He was no longer in the Government and felt he should not participate in the working out of detailed military plans for the blockade he had opposed. He did not return next day, going off, instead, to spend the week end at his farm in Maryland.

By Friday night there was broad agreement that the blockade would be the fittest, least provocative response open to the President. Again the question was raised whether blockading Cuba would be enough. Ted Sorensen had spent much of the day in his White House office trying to draft a speech for the President and making little progress. He had hoped that the labor of putting the blockade concept on paper would dispel his own doubts. Instead he found his mind cluttered with questions for which he knew no answer. He kept asking himself how a naval blockade in the waters surrounding Cuba would come to grips with the real problem of missiles on the island that, hour by hour, were nearing operational readiness. Stopping Russian ships at sea to make certain that they delivered no more missiles or bombers to Cuba seemed to him an attainable objective. But the blockade appeared wholly irrelevant to the threat from missiles already in place at San Cristóbal or Remedios, Guanajay or Sagua la Grande. He abandoned his writing to rejoin the committee in search of answers.

That night, thanks in part to Sorensen's questions, the blockade concept was refined by marrying it to the concept of further armed action, including an air strike, if it failed to dislodge the missiles in Cuba. "The consensus was emerging that we had to start with the blockade," Paul Nitze recalls. "It might or might not work. But if, after a reasonable period, we saw that the Russians were going ahead with their missile bases or uncrating the IL-28 bombers just delivered, then we would go to an air strike."

Sorensen went back to his desk, looked at the declaration-of-war speeches Woodrow Wilson and Franklin Roosevelt had delivered in 1917 and 1941, then started writing. By three o'clock Saturday morning, his first draft was ready for the President's scrutiny, along with the recommendation of the as yet unnamed Executive Committee.

That night, in the Sheraton Blackstone Hotel at Chicago, an uncomprehending Salinger heard Ken O'Donnell say: "The President may have to develop a cold tomorrow."

*Above all, while defending our own vital interests, nuclear powers must avert those confrontations which bring an adversary to the choice of either a humiliating retreat or a nuclear war.*
—JOHN F. KENNEDY, speaking at American University, Washington, D. C., June 10, 1963

PIERRE SALINGER, up at eight o'clock that Saturday morning, breakfasted in his Chicago hotel room before making his way downstairs. The Western Union manager, Carroll Linkins, stopped him in the press room with a message: the President wanted to see him right away. Salinger took the elevator to the Presidental suite, finding Kennedy with a slip of Sheraton Blackstone notepaper in his hand. On it, the President had written: "Slight upper respiratory [infection]. 1 degree temperature. Weather raw and rainy. Recommended return to Washington." Although he had been forewarned by O'Donnell Friday night, Salinger did not then question the President. Without knowing the primary reason, he felt that health was at best a secondary factor in the President's decision to break off his campaigning. At 9:35 A.M. central daylight time, he called the White House reporters together, gave them the story, and the whole caravan started back to the capital. On the plane, Salinger said to Kennedy: "There's nothing wrong with your health, is there, Mr. President?" Confirming that the illness was fictitious, Kennedy volunteered that something was about to happen. The President arrived back in the White House at

1:37 P.M., eastern daylight time. Nothing more was said except for Kennedy's instruction that Salinger should "stick around" in connection with the name-less something that was about to happen. "If you know nothing about it, you're lucky," the President said.

At 8:12 the same morning, the Joint Chiefs of Staff had sent a cautious signal to all the commanders in chief round the world, saying that unspecified tensions in Cuba could call for military action before long. The Caribbean and Atlantic commands had been alerted the previous day. But there was no telling where trouble would break out—Berlin, Iran, Turkey or the Far East. That morning (twelve hours earlier in New Delhi), there had been a flare-up on the Himalayan frontier between India and Red China. The Chinese accused the Indians of launching "a large-scale, frenzied attack" north of the disputed McMahon Line boundary. New Delhi reported that Chinese troops had overrun many Indian positions in the heaviest fighting since the border clashes had started three years earlier. Was this sheer coincidence? Or were the Chinese moving in co-ordination with the placement of Soviet missiles in Cuba?

At nine o'clock, the circle of Presidential advisers had met at the State Department and, with a few amendments, generally approved Sorensen's blockade speech. It was after this, at 10 A.M. eastern time, that Robert Kennedy had telephoned the President in Chicago, telling him to come home.

As McNamara was leaving the conference room that morning, the blockade recommendation just agreed upon, he grabbed a telephone, called the Pentagon and gave instructions that four tactical squadrons should be put in readiness for a possible air strike. To a startled State Department man, who could not avoid overhearing the conversation, the Secretary of Defense explained somewhat sheepishly:

"If the President doesn't accept our recommendation, there won't be time to do it later."

The die was cast when the President met with his Executive Committee in the Oval Room at 2:30 P.M. It was a long and—toward the end—an unexpectedly bitter session. The choices put before Kennedy that afternoon were two: begin with the naval blockade and, if need be, move up the ladder of military responses, rung by rung; or begin with an air strike, then move almost certainly to a full-scale invasion of Cuba. Dean Rusk had prepared a two-page summary in his own handwriting, carefully marked TOP SECRET. He read it to the assembled group, then handed the papers to the President, who handed them back. Rusk kept the document for his files. It recommended that the President choose the blockade track, while warning that this course would be neither safe nor comfortable, carrying with it the risks of rapid escalation. The Rusk document listed seven reasons for choosing blockade instead of the air strike he had argued for earlier. Of these, the most cogent was that the air strike would be an irreversible step. The blockade, by contrast, promised to keep other avenues open while providing time and opportunity for the Russians to reconsider carefully the dangers of their chosen course. McNamara also argued for blockade, saying that while either choice was risky, blockade appeared the more likely to achieve the removal of Soviet missiles from Cuba with the least risk.

The President paused gravely before speaking his mind. He said that he preferred to start with limited action. An air attack, he felt, was the wrong way to start. The modern bomber seemed to him hardly a surgical tool, but, rather, a blunt instrument. Before making his final decision he wanted to talk with the tactical bombing specialists. But the blockade, he felt, was the way to begin. He asked the air-strike advocates to understand that their alternative was by no means ruled out for the future. It might become necessary if the blockade failed in its purpose. For the moment, the blockade track had the advantage of preserving his own options and leaving some for Khrushchev. It applied enough pressure to make clear America's determination, but not so much as to force the Russians into desperate actions. Kennedy was still expecting a Soviet move against Berlin, whatever happened in Cuba. He inquired about the state of contingency planning for Berlin, then confessed that he was not happy with either alternative. "The ones whose plans we're not taking are the lucky ones," he said.

Adlai Stevenson, who had returned from New York for the decisive meetings, suggested that—simultaneous with the President's speech, already set for 7 P.M. Monday—the United States should call for an emergency session of the United Nations Security Council. Stevenson stressed the importance of getting in ahead of the Russians with a resolution that was acceptable to the United States. The President agreed. He also endorsed the plans Ed Martin had drafted for going to the Organization of American States. Stevenson had approved the blockade decision, insisting that OAS approval was vital. On Saturday afternoon he started thinking aloud about further diplomatic moves. The President, he urged, should consider offering to withdraw from the Guantánamo naval base as part of a plan to demilitarize, neutralize, and guarantee the territorial integrity of Cuba. Stevenson held that Guantánamo, in any event, was of little value. He also forecast grave difficulties concerning the Jupiter bases in Turkey. People would certainly ask why it was right for the United States to have bases in Turkey, but wrong for the Russians to have bases in Cuba. The President, he said, should consider offering to remove the Jupiters in exchange for the removal of Russian missiles from Cuba. Perhaps U.N. inspection teams could be set up to inspect all foreign bases, Russian as well as American, to guard against a surprise attack while the dismantling was being carried out.

Kennedy addressed himself directly to Stevenson's proposals, rejecting both. The United States, he said, simply could not at this stage consider giving up Guantánamo. As for the Jupiters, the President had his own doubts about their continued value and was willing to consider removing them in the right circumstances. But this was not the time for concessions that could wreck the Western alliance; seeming to confirm the suspicion Charles de Gaulle had planted that the United States would sacrifice the interests of its allies to protect its own security. Dillon, Lovett and McCone sharply attacked Stevenson, but the U.N. Ambassador stood his ground. This was the exchange that later led to published charges that "Adlai wanted a Munich." In fairness to Stevenson, Paul Nitze submits that as Ambassador to the United Nations, "Adlai had to be the one who looked at this proposition from the U.N. standpoint, the standpoint of simple equities and the hazards of war." Dean Rusk's impression is that Stevenson was not in fact advocating an American withdrawal from Guantánamo or from Turkey. He was trying to suggest what kinds of demands might be raised if, as many others also expected, the Russians dragged their feet after agreeing to remove the missiles from Cuba and thus involved the United States in a long, wearying negotiation.

Stevenson's own recollection was that he argued the United States ought to be willing to pay some price for the neutralization of Cuba if that meant getting the Russians out, along with their missiles. The bitter aftertaste of that Saturday afternoon in the Oval Room stayed with him until his death. It was after this encounter that Robert Kennedy decided Stevenson lacked the toughness to deal effectively with the Russians at the U.N. in liquidating the missiles crisis. He suggested to the President that John McCloy or Herman Phleger, the California Republican who had served as chief legal adviser to John Foster Dulles, be asked to help in the U.N. negotiations. McCloy got the job.

Instead of abandoning Guantánamo, orders went out that day to reinforce it. At El Toro, the Marine Corps air station south of Los Angeles, more than 1,000 leathernecks of the 2nd battalion, 1st Marine Division, were jumping out of the trucks that had brought them from Camp Pendleton. Jet transports of the Military Air Transport Service were standing by. And as night snuffed out the red glare of the setting sun over the Pacific, the transports loaded with marines in battle dress took off one by one for the big naval base in Cuba.

At Fort Hood, Texas, late Saturday night, units of the 1st Armored Division (Old Ironsides), U. S. Army, were routed from their beds. Suddenly the barracks came alive. Troopers scooped combat gear from their lockers into duffle bags and marched to the motor pools under the floodlights. In twenty-four hours the division was on its way to Fort Stewart, Georgia, a battalion at a time, tanks, personnel carriers and howitzers loaded on flatcars, men packing the special trains. All artillery rounds were primed, adjusted, and ready to fire.

It was much the same with the U.S.S. *Stickell*, and her skipper, Commander Tracy Wilder. On Saturday afternoon, Wilder was at his home in Little Creek, Virginia, painting window frames, when the telephone rang. Mrs. Wilder was at church directing choir practice. Wilder climbed down from a stepladder to answer the phone. It was the squadron engineering officer speaking:

"You are to prepare at once to get under way for extended operations," he said.

"Where to?" Wilder asked.

"Classified. I can't tell you."

"Well, do I turn right or left at the lightship?"

"Right."

"Thanks."

Seven hours later the destroyer *Stickell* slid from her pier, loaded with ammunition, provisions and ten new movies for shipboard showing. As Wilder eased out of Hampton Roads, turning right at the lightship *Chesapeake*, he received a terse order: "Proceed south." In Hampton Roads, *Stickell's* sudden departure went unnoticed. With so many carriers and cruisers around, a destroyer more or less gets little attention there. Anyone who knew the *Stickell* crew could not have failed to notice a lot of new faces on board. With part of his own crew on leave, Wilder had borrowed twenty-five men from each of three other destroyers.

That night, as *Stickell* and other destroyers moved south to take up blockade stations in the Caribbean, Dean Rusk telephoned Dean Acheson at his farm in Sandy Spring, Maryland. Rusk explained to his former boss that the President had made his decision, adding that it was not the decision Acheson had favored. The President, moreover, had decided that Acheson—in spite of his misgivings about the blockade—was the man to tell de Gaulle. Would he fly to Paris on Sunday? The request reminded Acheson of a saying by Judge Oliver Wendell Holmes. "We all belong to the least exclusive club in the world," Holmes used to say. "But it's the club with the highest dues—the United States of America." With that out of the way, Rusk settled back to enjoy a cardboard container of soup at his desk. His wife, Virginia, had brought it from home. It was the nearest thing to a home-cooked meal the Secretary of State had tasted all week.

Livingston Merchant, former Ambassador to Canada, was tracked down at a Princeton football game on Saturday afternoon and told he was to go back to Ottawa on Sunday to brief Prime Minister Diefenbaker. Walter Dowling, the Ambassador to West Germany, happened to be in Georgia on a visit to his ailing mother. He was summoned to Washington so he could fly to Europe with Acheson the following day and deliver a personal message from Kennedy to Chancellor Adenauer. That night the President telephoned his old friend, Ambassador Ormsby Gore, inviting him to drop in for lunch Sunday.

The smell of crisis was in the autumn air and alert newsmen were tracking the scent. Alfred Friendly, managing editor of the Washington *Post*, had heard something at a cocktail party that prompted him to send his best reporters to prowl the State Department corridors. Scotty Reston of the New York *Times* had been doing some prowling on his own. That night he called first George Ball and then McGeorge Bundy. It was clear that Reston had most of the essential facts. Both officials urged him, in the interests of national security, not to print what he knew. Reston agreed. The whole of official Washington respected Reston's nose for news. "This town being what it is," Ball recalled after the crisis, "I marveled that it should have taken Scotty Reston, of all people, five days to discover what was going on."

*By this time tomorrow, Gentlemen, we will be
in a flaming crisis.*
—DEAN RUSK to his staff, October 21, 1962

As IF to make amends for the punishing heat of the
Washington summer, October brought a succession
of golden autumn days, with a crisp foretaste of winter in the air. The President and Mrs. Kennedy went
to mass that glorious Sunday morning at St. Stephen's Church. White House reporters remarked that
for a man who had just cut short his political campaign, pleading illness, Kennedy looked surprisingly
fit.

Even before going to church, the President had
confirmed the blockade decision. The diehard advocates of direct armed action, once overruled, were
still arguing that blockade—in the words of Mc-
George Bundy—was a form of "slow agony" which
might fail in its prime purpose of dislodging the
Soviet missiles in Cuba. So the President called the
experts to his living quarters early that morning for
a final review of the air-strike alternative.

His brother, the Attorney General, was there, along
with McNamara, Maxwell Taylor, and a gaggle of
Air Force officers. The President asked General Walter
C. Sweeney, commander of the Tactical Air Force,
whether he could be certain that an air strike would
take out all the Soviet missiles at one stroke. Sweeney
replied that it should be possible to destroy some
90 per cent of them, though he could not guarantee
100 per cent effectiveness. A clean surgical operation,

in short, was a military impossibility. The plan called
for bombing Castro's military airports, as well as the
missile bases, and several of these were in populated
areas. Haunted by the thought that thousands of
Cuban civilians might be killed, in addition to the
Russians manning the missile sites, Kennedy once
again vetoed the air strike. Even if only 10 per cent
of the missile sites were to survive, he reasoned,
they might be fired against the United States.

At the State Department, the wire-service reporters
assigned to Sunday duty noticed the sign-in book
had disappeared from the reception desk at the diplomatic entrance. This minor departure from routine,
designed to conceal the comings and goings of high
officials, was enough to alert the reporters. They
started patrolling the corridors. The President's
secret would not keep much longer.

Donald May of United Press International surprised Pierre Salinger, with Robert Manning and
Arthur Sylvester, the information chiefs of the State
and Defense Departments, at a quiet planning conference in Manning's sixth-floor office. They were,
in fact, drawing up plans for the great disclosure
next day.

Salinger had been told what was up just that morning. After McGeorge Bundy outlined the dimensions
of the crisis, Kennedy said to Salinger: "Now, aren't
you glad you didn't know about this?"

Total concealment was out of the question at this
late stage. Too many reporters had seen too many
lights burning too late in unexpected places. Too
many senior officials had suddenly sent regrets to
dinner hostesses. The Administration decided its only
recourse was to confuse the reporters by laying down
a false scent. As a result, Averell Harriman (then
Assistant Secretary of State for Far Eastern Affairs)
was sent over to the White House in his big black
limousine with orders to make himself visible. Martin
Hillenbrand, of the German Affairs Office, and Philips

Talbot, Assistant Secretary of State for Near Eastern Affairs, got the same instructions.

All this public traffic at the West wing of the White House started some newsmen speculating about possible crises involving China, India or Berlin. Harriman, who did not much care for the decoy role, grumbled: "How long do I have to sit here?" Meanwhile, members of the Executive Committee came and went in total secrecy through a basement passageway leading from the Treasury Department on Fifteenth Street through the White House bomb shelters into the Oval Room.

There was another deliberate piece of official deception later in the day when newsmen started badgering Sylvester about a military exercise called Philbriglex-62, which was about to begin in the Caribbean. A force of some 7,500 marines, supported by four aircraft carriers, some 20 destroyers, and 15 troop carriers, was to storm the coral beaches of Vieques Island, off the southeast coast of Puerto Rico. The marines were to liberate a mythical Republic of Vieques from the tyranny of a mythical dictator named Ortsac—that is, Castro spelled backward.

Questioned about the real purpose of this exercise, Sylvester again took occasion to deny "that any alert has been ordered or that any emergency military measures have been set in motion against Communist-ruled Cuba." Philbriglex-62, he said, was just a big training exercise, having "nothing to do with any possible imminent action against Cuba."

Technically, Sylvester was telling the truth. Philbriglex-62 had been set in motion—and invitations had been issued to newsmen—before the missiles in Cuba were discovered. This was, of course, a narrow construction of the truth. Sylvester later argued the national interest was better served by keeping the Russians guessing at that moment than by fully informing the American people. It is hard to see how he could have done otherwise.

Dean Acheson, summoned from his Sandy Spring farm, had reached the State Department at eight o'clock on Sunday morning with his secretary of thirty years, Barbara Evans. She raced off to get Acheson's passport validated, then to raise some pocket money. The banks, of course, were closed. Miss Evans managed to borrow $60, the chief contributor being Ambassador Dowling. Then, while Miss Evans went to the Acheson house in Georgetown to pack a bag, her boss was told of the Presidential decision, briefed on his unexpected mission to Paris, and handed a letter from Kennedy for President de Gaulle. By midmorning Acheson was on his way with Ambassador Dowling, who was to be dropped in Germany so he could brief Chancellor Adenauer.

The Air Force jet set out over the Atlantic, its first stop to be a Strategic Air Command base at Greenham Common, near Newbury, England. David K. E. Bruce, Ambassador to the Court of St. James's, would be waiting there. In addition to Acheson and Dowling, the Boeing 707 carried Sherman Kent of the CIA, three sets of aerial photographs, three photo reconnaissance experts, and three armed guards. Acheson and Dowling spent part of their time studying the photographs. Whenever an Air Force crewman walked past, the CIA guards quickly covered the photographs.

In the Oval Room of the White House, the Executive Committee met at ten o'clock. Each of its members had a slip of paper in his pocket. It was Bobby Kennedy who had suggested that each man bring his own recommendation, in writing, to the Sunday session. When the President heard about this, he told his brother: "I'm going to let them keep those papers. Then those who disagree with me can prove they were right all along." The slips were never collected.*

* Paul Nitze, then Assistant Secretary of Defense for international security affairs, saved his slip of paper. It reads: "We

At the President's request, Douglas Dillon had delayed his scheduled Saturday departure for Mexico
City, where he was to speak for the United States at
the annual inter-American conference of Finance
Ministers on the Alliance for Progress. Kennedy had
come to lean heavily on Dillon's judgment and experience. So the Secretary of the Treasury, a Republican holdover from the Eisenhower Administration, sat in the Sunday morning meeting, helping to
review Sorensen's draft of the quarantine speech. Edwin Martin, the able, methodical Assistant Secretary
of State for Inter-American Affairs, estimated that
with 24 hours' advance notice the Organization of
American States could be counted upon to approve
the quarantine by 14 votes, the necessary two-thirds
majority. If the vote were held off 48 hours, Martin
predicted, the affirmative majority would go up
to 17.

As the Executive Committee members were going
through Sorensen's third speech draft, line by line,
there was talk of recasting it to hold Fidel Castro
more or less equally responsible with Nikita Khrushchev for the threat to peace in the Americas. George
Ball saw some merit in the idea of spreading the
onus. He felt it might "give the Russians a face-
saver if they were looking for one." There was, however, one obstacle. If Castro were to be arraigned
alongside Khrushchev, the blockade would have to
be extended to bar petroleum shipments and other
cargo important to the Cuban economy. McNamara

---

should follow the blockade with the offer of a political plan
in the UN. If in two or three days we have continuing evidence of progress (on the Soviet missile bases) we should
strike on a minimum number of targets. I believe it highly
unlikely the Soviets would strike SAC, with SAC fully alerted.
If the surviving missiles were used against us, I would invade
Cuba, without nuclear weapons. We might then have to make
a purely compensatory attack on the Soviet Union. I do not
believe effective action against the missiles in Cuba compli-
cates the Berlin problem. If we permit this to go unanswered,
we will be accepting coexistence on Khrushchev's terms."

argued the purpose of the blockade was, and should remain, uncomplicated: to get the missiles out of Cuba. His view prevailed. The Executive Committee agreed the first objective of the blockade must be to block further shipments of offensive military equipment to Cuba; the second, to see the missiles already in Cuba removed. •

Adlai Stevenson raised objections to the language of the Sorensen draft calling on the Russians to "render the missiles inoperable." He argued the President should be quite explicit in demanding that the Russians *dismantle* and *remove* their missiles. There was some danger, he felt, that the Russians might announce they had "rendered the missiles inoperable" and then balk at removing them. "I assumed," Stevenson later recalled, "that the Russians, given the threat of nuclear war, would stall and try to keep the missiles in place. Then we would be in for a long, hard, bargaining session."

It was a few minutes before noon, with the Executive Committee still in session, when David Ormsby Gore, the British Ambassador, arrived at the White House. He waited a half hour until the President was free. Kennedy lost no time telling his old friend what was happening in Cuba; though, typically, he did not disclose what actions had been decided upon. He outlined the various alternatives: air strike, blockade or going to the United Nations and putting the facts on the table. "What would you do?" Kennedy asked.

Forced to improvise, Ormsby Gore discussed the alternatives briefly. He saw no merit in the air-strike idea. There might be an immediate Soviet riposte in Berlin; moreover, it would be hard to persuade public opinion that the United States was behaving like a reasonable, responsible power if it struck without warning. The British Ambassador also dismissed the United Nations approach, on the ground that it would not come to grips quickly enough with the real prob-

lem represented by Soviet missiles in Cuba. Having
eliminated these alternatives, Ormsby Gore spoke out
for blockade. It seemed, he said, the sensible alternative. At this Kennedy grinned broadly.

"You'll be happy to know that's what we are going
to do," the President said. The two went in to lunch;
then sat together on the Truman balcony, enjoying
the splendor of the October sun. Kennedy said he
would be telephoning Macmillan that evening. At the
President's request, the Ambassador speculated about
the likely reaction of Macmillan and Lord Home,
then Foreign Secretary. Toward midafternoon, Ormsby Gore returned to the British Embassy on Massachusetts Avenue. There, he drafted and dispatched
a long, detailed report for the Prime Minister on the
crisis that was now just a few hours away.* If the
British Government was not consulted, it certainly
was informed before any other ally.

At 2:30 P.M. the National Security Council held
its first formal meeting of the missiles crisis to ratify
the decisions already hammered out in the smaller
Executive Committee. It was there that some Cabinet members heard for the first time of the great
confrontation ahead. Donald Wilson, then deputy director of the United States Information Agency,
joined the group in the place of his ailing boss, Edward R. Murrow.

Admiral George W. Anderson, Chief of Naval Operations, outlined his plans for the blockade and the
first interception of Soviet vessels bound for Cuba.
Once the blockade decision had been ratified, President Kennedy turned to Anderson.

"This is up to the Navy," he said.

---

* That evening, Ormsby Gore returned to the White House
for a small dinner with the Kennedys and a few friends.
Jacqueline Kennedy felt a relaxed evening at home was what
the President needed. Talk of Cuba or missiles was taboo. "We
tried all through dinner to keep off the subject," Ormsby
Gore recalls. "But it was awkward. There was just too much
tension in the room."

Anderson replied: "Mr. President, the Navy won't let you down."

With these formalities out of the way, Dillon left for Mexico in the Presidential jet plane. The plane deposited him in the care of Thomas Mann, then United States Ambassador in Mexico City. The pilot had to fly back at once to start picking up Congressional leaders of both parties at various points across the country. (Most Congressmen were in their home states busily campaigning when the President decided to call the leaders back to Washington for a briefing on Monday afternoon. Lawrence F. O'Brien, Kennedy's chief of Congressional liaison, reached nineteen of them on the telephone during the day. All he could tell the leaders was: "The President wants you to come.")

As soon as he could get Mann off by himself, Dillon told him what was about to happen. Mann confessed that, though he had spent much of the past week in Washington, he knew nothing about the crisis. They decided that their Mexican hosts should, as a courtesy, be told in advance of President Kennedy's decision. President Lopez Mateos of Mexico was on a state visit to the Philippines with his Foreign Minister. So Dillon and Mann decided the man to approach was Mexico's Finance Minister, Ortiz Mena.

Back in Washington, the State Department was in a fever of preparations. Top-secret telegrams were drafted and coded for transmission to all American ambassadors round the world, outlining the proposed course of action. The text of the President's speech, with a covering letter to Premier Khrushchev, in code, was dispatched to the American Embassy in Moscow. (These were to be delivered one hour before the President's speech on Monday evening—that is, at 6 P.M. Washington time, October 22.) Apart from the letters to de Gaulle, Adenauer, and Diefenbaker—already en route in the hands of Acheson, Dowling, and Merchant—Presidential letters were dispatched through the embassies to Macmillan, Nehru, Premier Fanfani of Italy, and Mayor Brandt of West Berlin—altogether to forty-three heads of government.

Dean Rusk checked all the preparations, sighed audibly, and advised his staff to get some sleep. "By this time tomorrow, Gentlemen," the Secretary of State said, "we will be in a flaming crisis."

At the Pentagon, across the Potomac, the Joint Chiefs of Staff issued a stream of directives: to the Commander in Chief, Atlantic, to prepare for the evacuation of all dependents from Guantánamo naval base the following day; to various area commanders assigning them operational control of specified Army and Air Force units.

At 10 P.M. Washington time, McNamara approved the quarantine procedures, the rules under which the Navy was to operate in the Caribbean encounter. He also authorized Air Force interceptors flying in the United States to carry nuclear weapons.

The troop movements, however, were beginning to draw public attention. Both the Washington *Post* and the New York *Times* had put together a fairly shrewd notion of what was coming. So the President telephoned Orvil Dryfoos, then publisher of the *Times*, and Philip Graham, publisher of the *Post*, asking them not to give the game away in Monday morning's newspapers. McNamara made a similar appeal to John Hay Whitney, publisher of the New York *Herald Tribune*.

Publishing less than it knew, the *Times* that night carried a front-page story about preparations for an unspecified major crisis. The story read, in part:

WASHINGTON, October 21—There was an air of crisis in the capital tonight.

President Kennedy and the highest Administration officials have been in almost constant conference all weekend, imparting serious agitation and tension to official Washington.

Mr. Kennedy is expected to go on television to give the country an explanation in the next day or two, but he has wrapped a tight veil of secrecy around the source of his concern so far.

Coincidentally, the Navy and Marine Corps were staging a powerful show of force in the Caribbean, not far from Cuba, which has been the site of a large Communist build-up in recent weeks.

The Administration denies that there is any connection between the anxious mood here and these maneuvers, which involve about 20,000 men, including 6,000 marines.

But the speculation in Washington was that there has been a new development in Cuba that cannot be disclosed at this point. . . .

Long after dark, Ambassador Bruce was waiting at Greenham Common when the Acheson plane whistled in from Washington. Bruce had not been told whom he would be meeting there. But, with characteristic thoughtfulness, he had brought a quart of Scotch. Acheson accepted it gratefully, as he dropped off one set of aerial photographs, one security man, and one photo-interpreter. Bruce was to show Macmillan the evidence next morning. The courtly Ambassador whispered to Acheson: "Put your hand in my coat pocket." Acheson did so and his fingers closed round a service revolver. Bruce explained that he had borrowed it from a marine guard at the American Embassy in Grosvenor Square when he had received the somewhat mystifying instructions to be at Greenham Common that night, alone and armed. Bruce had been Ambassador to France when Acheson was Secretary of State. They were old friends and the laugh they joined in took the edge off their tension.

Acheson flew on to France, landing past midnight at Evreux, where he was met by Cecil Lyon, then

the American Minister in Paris, and Thomas K. Finletter, U. S. Ambassador to the North Atlantic Council. He reached Paris about 2:30 A.M., fell into bed
and was barely flirting with sleep when there was a
call from Washington. The President wanted him to
go on to Germany to reassure Adenauer, after seeing
de Gaulle. Acheson agreed and turned back gratefully to his pillow.

*A great government such as yours does not act
without evidence.*
—CHARLES DE GAULLE to Dean Acheson,
Paris, October 22, 1962

WHILE WASHINGTON SLEPT, Ambassador David Bruce
in London went to Admiralty House with the photographs Dean Acheson had confided to his care at
Greenham Common. Prime Minister Macmillan had
known of the crisis since Friday. He was seeing for
the first time that Monday morning the evidence that
had prompted the President's action. The Prime Minister had long been haunted by the nightmare vision
of a world blasted by nuclear weaponry out of control. The week of October 22, he said later, "was
the week of most strain I can ever remember in my
life." Any man of normal intelligence could see the
danger that, for the first time since Hiroshima and
Nagasaki, the poisonous mushroom cloud might at
any moment be loosed over a great city. Macmillan
was endowed with a keener intelligence and a more
vivid imagination than most men. He examined the
photographs soberly as Bruce's photo-interpreter
pointed out the missiles, the launch-erectors, and the
fuel trucks scattered over the Cuban landscape. No
special pleading was required. "I take it for granted,"
Macmillan said, "that the statements made by your
government are unchallengeable."

In Paris that morning, Acheson briefed the American mission to NATO. Then at five o'clock (it was
11 A.M. in Washington), he slipped through a side

entrance into the Elysée Palace. The interview with de Gaulle was graced by a regal courtesy on both sides. "Your President does me great honor," de Gaulle said, "to send me so distinguished an emissary. I assume the occasion to be of appropriate importance." Acheson delivered President Kennedy's letter, with the text of the speech to be delivered at P-hour, 7 P.M. Washington time. He offered to summarize it. De Gaulle raised his hand in a delaying gesture that the long-departed Kings of France might have envied. "May we be clear before you start," he said. "Are you consulting or informing me?" Acheson confessed that he was there to inform, not consult. "I am in favor of independent decisions," de Gaulle acknowledged.

When Acheson completed his summary, de Gaulle lost no time groping for the right words. "It is exactly what I would have done," he said. Then Acheson offered to show the photographs. De Gaulle swept them aside. "A great government such as yours does not act without evidence," he said. The two talked of Soviet responses, reviewing the possibility of a riposte in Berlin or Turkey. Acheson assured de Gaulle that these dangers had been foreseen; the United States was prepared to deal with them. De Gaulle predicted the situation would not arise. "You may tell your President that France will support him," he said. "I think that under the circumstances President Kennedy had no other choice. This is his national prerogative and France understands."

Only then did de Gaulle ask to see the photographs. The old soldier slumbering beneath the dark, double-breasted suit of the President of the Republic wakened to this new marvel of military intelligence. He inquired from what altitude the pictures had been taken. Acheson told him 14 miles. "C'est formidable," de Gaulle exclaimed. "C'est formidable." In the sheaf of photographs was one showing a concentration of MIG fighter planes parked on a Cuban airfield. Four models were visible—the MIG 15, MIG 17, MIG 19 and the latest MIG 21. Acheson's companion, Sherman Kent of the CIA, invited de Gaulle to identify them. Delighted, the old general put a magnifying glass to the photograph. In spite of failing vision he managed to sort out four separate models of the Soviet fighter plane, though he confessed that he could not say which was which. De Gaulle then asked Acheson why, in his view, the Russians had put missiles into Cuba. Acheson replied that he believed Khrushchev had gambled. The answer might not be flattering to his own government, he said, but the Russians perhaps had been led to believe that they could get away with it. De Gaulle nodded in agreement.

Adenauer was informed the same day by Ambassador Dowling. In Ottawa, Livingston Merchant briefed the Canadian Prime Minister, John Diefenbaker. Of the four Allied leaders, Diefenbaker was the only one who showed a certain suspicion of the President's motives. He agreed, nevertheless, to deny Cuban or Russian planes landing rights at Gander Airport in Newfoundland.

In Frankfurt on the Main, John McCloy was sitting down to an important business conference when Washington called. "Sorry, boys," McCloy said to his business associates. "I hate to drop names, but the President needs me." McCloy caught the next plane home to begin work with Adlai Stevenson at the United Nations.

That morning in Washington, the Joint Chiefs of Staff issued a blockade-planning directive to the Atlantic Fleet. Air Force missile crews both at home and overseas got their "Maximum alert" orders. Men assigned to intercontinental ballistic missile sites in the Western states, capable of launching a devastating counterstrike against Russia, went on a 70-hour work-week. As of October 22, 156 ICMs were ready to be fired. At noon, from his underground headquarters at Offutt Air Force Base, near Omaha, General

Thomas S. Power of the Strategic Air Command started dispersing his B-47 bombers to 40 civilian airports in various parts of the country. General Power was taking no chances with a possible Soviet missile attack on his permanent bases. All bomb-bay doors were shut, signifying that each plane carried its assigned load of nuclear bombs. The same day the SAC commander ordered his B-52 bomber force into the air. For thirty days and nights to follow, part of the B-52 force was in the air at all times. It was the biggest airborne alert in SAC's history. As one B-52 landed, another would take its place in the sky. Every plane on the ground carried its full load of fuel and bombs, ready to take off on fifteen minutes' warning. Five Army divisions, not counting the 1st Armored (already on its way to Fort Stewart, Georgia), were on alert orders. The Navy had deployed 180 ships in the Caribbean, including the special blockade task force of destroyers, backed by cruisers. It was the swiftest, smoothest military build-up in the history of the United States, with every major unit in position before the President addressed the country and the world.

At noon on Monday, Pierre Salinger called Robert Fleming of the American Broadcasting Company, the pool co-ordinator that month for the three television networks. He told Fleming that the President would speak at seven o'clock on "a matter of highest national urgency," nothing more.

At 11:30 that morning the President had met briefly with the Executive Committee to approve the final draft of his speech and button up other procedural details. Abram Chayes, the State Department legal adviser, suggested a language change. Instead of basing the blockade on Article 51 of the United Nations Charter, which assures each nation's inherent right of self-defense in case of armed attack, Chayes argued that its legal basis should be the right of the OAS to take collective measures in guarding the se-

curity of the Americas. To an international lawyer
the distinction had its importance in avoiding the establishment of a self-defense precedent the Russians
might use in the future. This was quickly accepted.
The President also adopted Leonard Meeker's suggestion that the blockade should be styled a "defensive quarantine." Meeker and Chayes had argued
that the word "blockade" carried ugly, warlike over-
tones.

At three o'clock, after a quick swim in the White
House pool and a private lunch in the family dining room, Kennedy held a second formal meeting with
the National Security Council. The chief business
transacted was to give a name to the President's circle
of crisis advisers, who at various times until that day
had been called the War Cabinet, the War Council,
or just "the Group." In four hours the need for secrecy would pass. So the Security Council approved
Action Memorandum 196, formally establishing an
Executive Committee "for the purpose of effective
conduct of the operations of the executive branch in
the current crisis." The President would act as chairman. Until further notice, the Executive Committee
was to meet with him at ten o'clock each morning
in the Cabinet Room.

Its membership also was listed:

The Vice President, the Secretary of State, the Secretary of Defense, the Secretary of the Treasury, the
Attorney General, the director of the Central Intelligence Agency (McCone), the Under Secretary of
State (Ball), the Deputy Secretary of Defense (Gilpatric), the Chairman of the Joint Chiefs of Staff
(General Taylor), the Ambassador at Large (Thompson), the Special Counsel (Sorensen), and the Special Assistant to the President for national security
affairs (McGeorge Bundy).

There was some talk after the christening ceremony
about steps to be taken in the event a U-2 plane

was shot down over Cuba. With six or seven overflights a day now the rule, and the SAM sites in
Cuba about to become operational, this was no longer
a remote possibility. As the meeting broke up, the
President cautioned everyone against revealing that
an air strike or an invasion of Cuba was being considered, should the blockade not succeed in removing the Soviet missiles. Vice President Johnson, Rusk,
McNamara, and Robert Kennedy stayed behind for
a Cabinet meeting at four o'clock. Only then, a full
week after the San Cristóbal discovery, was the rest
of the Cabinet informed.

In Mexico City that afternoon, Dillon disclosed the
President's plan to his host, the Mexican Finance Minister. He delivered at the same time a letter for President Lopez Mateos, who was on his way back from a
visit to the Philippines. Dillon explained that Kennedy felt he had no choice but to take all necessary
action to repel "this invasion of the hemisphere by a
foreign power." He expressed the hope that the Mexican Government would understand and approve the
President's actions. Finance Minister Ortiz Mena assured him that Mexico understood this was not merely
a quarrel with Fidel Castro but a serious challenge
from Russia. Mexico, he said, will be at your side.
Dillon felt it was "a very brave and moving thing"
that Ortiz had said on his own authority.

Over the week end, Don Wilson had put together
his Spanish-language radio network, at least on paper.
The President's speech would be heard in Cuba
through the combined facilities of three Miami sta-
tions, WMIE, WGBS and WCKR; station WKWF,
Key West; WSB, Atlanta; WCKY, Cincinnati; WWL,
New Orleans; two short-wave stations, WRUL in
New York and KGEI in San Carlos, California, and
Radio Americas (formerly called Swan Radio), a CIA
transmitter operating from an island in the Gulf of
Mexico. The telephone company had cleared lines to
each of them for P-hour. A single detail remained

to be dealt with: not one of the station managers had yet been informed that his facilities were about to be borrowed by the Government. Wilson left that job to Pierre Salinger. At 6 P.M., Wilson and Newton Minow, chairman of the Federal Communications Commission, were in Salinger's office with a list of managers or station owners to be called. The White House switchboard put in nine calls, and Salinger, reading from a prepared paper, requested the cooperation of each station in turn. It was a project, Salinger said, "of the highest national importance": Beginning at seven o'clock the Government wanted to use their facilities for an indefinite period. Each one agreed and by 6:20 P.M. Wilson had his Spanish-language network ready to carry the President's speech into Cuba. Forty minutes later, the network started broadcasting.

It was a day of perpetual alarms, starting with a report from New York that Andrei Gromyko, the Soviet Foreign Minister, would have an important statement for the press before flying home to Moscow that afternoon. As soon as that word reached Washington, some officials came down with galloping jitters. They feared the Russians had somehow discovered what was about to happen, and would try in some undefined way to derail the President's big move. A contingency plan was whipped up to announce the blockade before seven o'clock if necessary. Salinger in fact alerted the reporters and cameramen, who were milling about in the west lobby of the White House. Gromyko's "important statement," piped into the White House from Idlewild Airport, turned out to be the customary string of farewell clichés. A second attack of official nerves started with the report of a Soviet Ilyushin-18 prop-jet headed in the direction of Cuba. There were solemn consultations about whether it should be allowed to land or warned off. This, too, was exposed as a false alarm when word arrived that the airliner was on its way to Brazil to fly home the body of the Soviet Ambassador to Rio de Janeiro, who had drowned a few days earlier.

These rumors and alarms left the President untroubled. His most difficult moment of the day came when he met with the Congressional leaders at five o'clock. Kennedy had spent six years in the House of Representatives, eight in the Senate. Yet his relations with the Congress were never easy. On this occasion, the President asked McCone to disclose the evidence. Then Rusk and McNamara explained what steps were being taken to deal with the threat. The President had expected the Republicans to be sourly suspicious. He was not prepared to hear the Democrats question his course, as two of the most respected leaders of his own party in Congress promptly did.

Senator Russell, the Georgia Democrat, dismissed the blockade as a halfway measure that would irritate the Allies while doing the Communists no tangible harm. Senator Fulbright of Arkansas, Chairman of the Foreign Relations Committee, shook the President by supporting Russell's demand for an invasion. This was the same Fulbright who had opposed the Bay of Pigs landing with the argument: "The Castro regime is a thorn in the flesh; but it is not a dagger in the heart." His inconsistency was, however, more apparent than real. In recommending against the 1961 landing, Fulbright had argued for a policy of tolerating and isolating Castro, with one proviso: "that the Soviet Union uses Cuba only as a political and not as a military base." His memorandum to the President, dated March 29, 1961, defined "military" as meaning a base for "missiles and nuclear weapons, not small conventional arms." * Now that Cuba had become such a military base, the Arkansas Senator was able to claim a certain logical consistency. Kennedy was angry—angrier with the invasion demand of

* *Fulbright of Arkansas: The Public Positions of a Private Thinker,* edited by Karl E. Meyer; Robert B. Luce, Inc. 1963.

Russell and Fulbright than with the expected declaration of Congressman Halleck of Indiana, then Republican leader of the House of Representatives, that
while he would support the blockade he wanted the
record to show that he had been informed, not consulted. As a group, the Congressional leaders felt
the blockade route would certainly be slow, probably
ineffective in coming to grips with the missiles in
Cuba, and perhaps more dangerous than a quick invasion. The President felt they were carping. He emphasized that the quarantine was a first step, that an
invasion might become necessary before the crisis was
resolved and that he was acting on his own authority,
after a solid week of carefully reviewing the alternatives. Kennedy left the room, having spent more
than an hour with the Congressional leaders, in a
smoldering rage.

Alexis Johnson's master scenario had specified
every step of the informing process in meticulous detail. At 6 o'clock, one hour before the President was
to speak, Rusk was back in his State Department office to break the news to the Soviet Ambassador.
Dobrynin, who had been in New York earlier that
day to see Gromyko off to Moscow, arrived on time,
smiling easily as he exchanged small talk with the
reporters at the diplomatic entrance. He left after
twenty-five minutes looking grim-faced and shaken.
Rusk had given Dobrynin a copy of the President's
speech, reading aloud portions of the text. There was
not much he needed to add. It was a somber conversation with no outbursts on either side. Both men
were professionals. On his way out, a reporter
asked Dobrynin whether there was a new crisis. "Ask
the Secretary," he said, racing toward his car. "You
can judge for yourself."

At 6:15, George Ball started briefing forty-six ambassadors of allied countries in the State Department's
international conference room. As the ambassadors
poured into the lobby, many carrying attaché cases,

some grumbled that the United States might have told them sooner. Many of the ambassadors from North Atlantic Treaty countries, and from those belonging to the Central Treaty Organization or the South-East Asian Treaty Organization, stayed behind to watch the President's speech on television. As they waited, a savings and loan commercial flashed on the screen. "How much security does your family have?" the announcer asked. The ambassadors, who had been gloomily weighing the dangers of nuclear war in a matter of hours, found the question hilariously appropriate. They roared with laughter.

In the President's study, at that moment, Kennedy was scanning his speech text when he heard a bustle in the adjoining room. Startled, he looked around to find Mrs. Lincoln, hairbrush in hand, advancing to recommend one final effort at taming his unruly hair. On cue from a network floorman, the President started speaking:

Good evening, my fellow citizens.

The Government, as promised, has maintained the closest surveillance of the Soviet military build-up on the island of Cuba. Within the past week, unmistakable evidence has established the fact that a series of offensive missile sites is now in preparation on that imprisoned island. The purpose of these bases can be none other than to provide a nuclear strike capability against the Western hemisphere. . . .

Several of them include medium-range ballistic missiles, capable of carrying a nuclear warhead for a distance of more than 1,000 nautical miles. Each of these missiles, in short, is capable of striking Washington, D.C., the Panama Canal, Cape Canaveral, Mexico City, or any other city in the Southeastern part of the United States, in Central America or in the Caribbean area.

Additional sites, not yet completed, appear to be designed for intermediate-range ballistic missiles— capable of travelling more than twice as far—and thus capable of striking most of the major cities in the

Western Hemisphere, ranging as far north as Hudson's Bay, Canada, and as far south as Lima, Peru. In addition, jet bombers, capable of carrying nuclear weapons, are now being uncrated and assembled in Cuba, while the necessary air bases are being prepared. . . .

With swift, sure strokes, Kennedy catalogued the long series of Soviet deceptions—the Kremlin's public and private assurances that only defensive weapons were going into Cuba, Gromyko's personal assurances and Khrushchev's boasts that Russian missiles were so powerful they could seek out any enemy, no matter how far removed, without the need for launching sites "beyond the boundaries of the Soviet Union." The President punctuated each Soviet declaration of peaceful intent with: "That statement was false," or, "That statement also was false." He blamed not Castro but the Soviet Union and clearly drew the line:

. . . this secret, swift and extraordinary build-up of Communist missiles—in an area well known to have a special and historical relationship to the United States and the nations of the Western Hemisphere, in violation of Soviet assurances, and in defiance of American and hemispheric policy—this sudden, clandestine decision to station strategic weapons for the first time outside of Soviet soil—is a deliberately provocative and unjustified change in the status quo which cannot be accepted by this country, if our courage and our commitments are ever to be trusted again by either friend or foe.

Recalling the lessons of appeasement in the Thirties, which as a student of twenty-three he had drawn in his first book, *Why England Slept*, Kennedy outlined his initial steps:

1. *The quarantine:* "All ships of any kind bound for Cuba from whatever nation or port will, if found to contain cargoes of offensive weapons, be turned back. . . . We are not at this time, however, denying

the necessities of life as the Soviets attempted to do in their Berlin blockade of 1948."

2. *Continued close surveillance:* "I trust that in the interests of both the Cuban people and the Soviet technicians at the sites, the hazards to all concerned of continuing this threat will be recognized."

3. *Retaliation:* "It shall be the policy of this nation to regard any nuclear missile launched from Cuba against any nation in the Western Hemisphere as an attack by the Soviet Union on the United States, requiring a full retaliatory response upon the Soviet Union."

4. *Guantánamo:* Wives and children of the Navy families have been evacuated and the base itself reinforced "as a necessary military precaution."

5. *Diplomatic action:* The Organization of American States is being asked to meet immediately to consider the threat to peace and to invoke the Rio Treaty.

6. *United Nations:* The United States is calling for an emergency meeting of the Security Council to approve a resolution that would require the Soviet Union to dismantle and promptly remove all offensive weapons from Cuba before the quarantine is lifted.

7. *Appeal to reason:* "I call upon Chairman Khrushchev to halt and eliminate this clandestine, reckless and provocative threat to world peace and to stable relations between our two nations. I call upon him further to abandon this course of world domination, and to join in an historic effort to end the perilous arms race and to transform the history of man. He has an opportunity now to move the world back from the abyss of destruction—by returning to his government's own words that it had no need to station missiles outside its own territory, and withdrawing these weapons from Cuba. . . ."

As the President spoke, a diplomatic reception was in progress at the Yugoslav mission to the United Nations in New York. The unhappy host, Ambassador

Misa Pavicevic, had turned on the television so his guests could see and hear Kennedy's speech. Fear of war gripped many of the listeners. Every step, Pavicevic said, "is taking us farther along the path we all deplore." At least one Yugoslav Communist paid Kennedy a kind of tribute: "I think he is right," he said. "He has almost convinced me."

At 7:30 P.M. Adlai Stevenson delivered to Ambassador Valerian Zorin of the Soviet Union, in his capacity as Chairman of the Security Council, a request that the Council meet urgently to deal with "the dangerous threat to the peace and security of the world caused by the secret establishment in Cuba . . . of launching bases and the installation of long-range ballistic missiles capable of carrying thermonuclear warheads to most of North and South America." Stevenson attached to his letter a four-part draft resolution that would have the Security Council call for the immediate dismantling and removal of missiles and bombers from Cuba; authorize the Acting Secretary General, U Thant, to send a United Nations Observer Corps to Cuba for the purpose of assuring and reporting on the withdrawal of offensive weapons; call for termination of the quarantine once the U.N. Observer Corps had certified the missiles were out of Cuba; and urgently recommend negotiations between the United States and the Soviet Union "on measures to remove the existing threat."

At the same hour, Ed Martin was briefing the Ambassadors of the Organization of American States. Dean Rusk had reserved for himself the difficult task of explaining the origins of the crisis to Ambassadors of the nonaligned and neutral countries, so prone in past Soviet-American confrontations to take a "plague on both your houses" attitude.

It is inconceivable to us how the Soviet leaders could have made so gross an error of judgment [Rusk said], with respect to our necessities, our strength or

our will. If we seem to be pointing the finger at the
Soviet Union rather more than at Cuba, it is because
we consider Cuba to be the victim of this situation.
Our information is that on these sites . . . Cubans
are not permitted to be present. Soviet guards bar
this area not only from Cuban civilians but from the
Cuban military.. . . .

I shall not, out of deference to you and to the complete independence of your great countries . . . attempt to persuade you to see it our way because,
Excellencies, this situation is one which causes each
nation, yours as well as ours, to look deeply at its
own most fundamental commitments. . . . This is not
a problem of balancing off one or the other. This re-
quires each of us—we, the Soviet Union, all of you—to
look at this situation in terms of national purposes,
national commitments, national interests. . . . I suggest to you that one of the issues that is involved here
is the independence of states. . . .

We do hope that the Soviet leaders, who made a
great error of judgment, will find some way to pull
back and to get back on the track of the peaceful
settlement of issues and disputes. But I would not be
candid and I would not be fair with you if I did not
say that we are in as grave a crisis as mankind has
been in, and this deeply affects the lives and fortunes
. . . of all of you represented in this room.

It was, as Rusk remembers it, a "very grave, very
sober" session. A considerable number of the neutral
or nonaligned Ambassadors stopped to shake his hand
on the way out, whispering that they now understood
why the United States had taken this momentous
decision and wishing the President good luck.

At the same hour, George Ball and McNamara held
separate briefings for the State Department and Pentagon correspondents. A reporter asked McNamara
how the Navy would challenge Soviet ships bound
for Cuba. "If they stop," he replied, "we will send a
boarding party on board, review the manifest, search
the cargo. In the event that there is no indication of

offensive weapons on board, the ship will proceed. If there is an indication of offensive weapons on board, the captain . . . will be given the option of proceeding to any port he chooses other than a port of Cuba. If he refuses to change his course, we will use force. . . ." In short, the Navy was ready to sink any Russian ship whose captain tried to run the blockade.

The ball was in Nikita Khrushchev's court. And no man could predict, with any assurance, how he would reply. Musing about Khrushchev's choices with an interviewer that Monday evening, George Ball ticked them off: "Is he going to abide by the quarantine that we are about to establish with our Latin American colleagues and allies? Is he going to try to run that quarantine, to break it? Is he going to try to reply somewhere else in the world?" Whatever Khrushchev may decide, Ball said gloomily: "We are prepared. We are prepared."

That night the Under Secretary of State slept fitfully on his office couch.

*We have won a considerable victory. You and
I are still alive.*
—DEAN RUSK to George Ball, October 23, 1962

GEORGE BALL, asleep on the davenport in his office
at the State Department, wakened to the sound of
approaching footsteps. It was the Secretary of State,
Dean Rusk, smiling as he had not smiled in days.
"We have won a considerable victory," Rusk said.
"You and I are still alive." Rusk had gone home late
Monday night without the vaguest intimation of
Khrushchev's likely response to the Cuban quarantine. That morning it became clear that the Secretary
of State's worst fears had not materialized. The Russians had not blocked the autobahn to Berlin. They
had not bombed the Jupiter bases in Turkey or
moved to close the Dardanelles. Taken by surprise,
the Kremlin leaders seemed to be stalling while they
considered their response. Rusk's initial impression
that Khrushchev had not decided what to do next
was confirmed in a few minutes. At eight o'clock on
Tuesday morning, thirteen hours after the Kennedy
speech, the Tass news agency started to transmit a
Soviet Government statement. It was a long statement, charging the President with piracy, "unheard
of violation of international law," and provocative
acts that might lead to thermonuclear war. There was
no hint of Soviet counteraction. Only indignant denials that Soviet missiles in Cuba served any but the
noblest of defensive purposes mixed with lofty
declarations of peaceful intent.

The Western Allies were standing firm behind the President. In New York, representatives of all other NATO governments received instructions to vote for the United States resolution in the Security Council. Prime Minister Macmillan telephoned Kennedy from London, pledging Britain's full support. In Bonn that morning, Dean Acheson called on Konrad Adenauer, who had shown traces of agitation when Ambassador Dowling had briefed him on Monday. By Tuesday, the aged Chancellor was once again stouthearted, his fears that the Russians would move instantly against Berlin apparently calmed. He had a great regard for Acheson as the original cold warrior. Adenauer amused his distinguished visitor by suggesting "various forms of skulduggery" by which the Russians could be further discomfited. Later that day Acheson talked with the German Defense Minister, Franz Joseph Strauss. He then flew home overnight to accept the President's gratitude for two delicate jobs of alliance diplomacy brilliantly accomplished.

In London, Ambassador Bruce was troubled by the initial reaction of the big British national newspapers. The *Daily Mail*, true-blue Conservative in politics, called the blockade "an act of war." Its front-page editorial was calculated to undermine public support for Kennedy. "The world cannot help fearing," the *Mail* said, "that in thus advancing to the brink of war, President Kennedy may have been led more by popular emotion than by calm statesmanship. . . . The perilous trend of events now set in motion must be halted before it is too late." The *Guardian*, traditionally Liberal, predicted a Soviet countermove against the Jupiter bases in Turkey. "In the end," said the *Guardian*, "the United States may find it has done its cause, its friends and its own true interests little good." The *Daily Telegraph*, Conservative, conceded that Britons could "sympathize with the President's refusal to condone a military build-up at his

back door." But, the *Telegraph* clucked, "he has surprised more than his enemies by the announcement."
Disappointed by the press reaction, Bruce set about
persuading Washington to release the U-2 photographs for publication in the newspapers and on
British television. Let those who doubt the President's right to act, the Ambassador argued, see for
themselves that he acted with good reason against
a real danger.

At 9 A.M. Washington time, Dean Rusk was in the
United States chair at the Organization of American States, hoping by his personal participation to
better Ed Martin's estimate that with luck the blockade would get fourteen approving votes, the bare
minimum required. Collective action under the Rio
Treaty called for a two-thirds' majority of the 21
American republics. Cuba, of course, was not par-
ticipating, but the magic number remained 14. Rusk
stressed the dangers that Latin America, for the first
time in history, was sharing with the United States:

These new weapons arriving in Cuba are not only
directed against the United States. Let there be no
misunderstanding. There are other strategic targets in
this hemisphere—in your countries—which they can
devastate with their lethal loads. . . . In the face of
this rapid build-up, no country of this hemisphere can
feel secure either from direct attack or from persistent blackmail.

Rusk explained that, whatever the United Nations
Security Council might decide in New York, the
American Republics had the primary responsibility
to act in defense of the hemisphere. "Without awaiting the outcome of the United Nations approach,"
he pleaded, "we must ensure that our hemisphere is
effectively quarantined against any further additions
to Soviet offensive nuclear military power in our
midst." Among international organizations the OAS
Council had long been notorious for preferring flow-

ery talk to action. This time the Latin ambassadors rose to the occasion, swept along by a rare feeling of solidarity through shared danger.

Dispensing with the ceremonious flourishes that are characteristic of OAS speeches, Latin ambassador after Latin ambassador spoke simply and strongly in support of Rusk's resolution authorizing the use of force, individually or collectively, in a blockade of Cuba. Ed Martin's forecast was soon revealed to be unduly pessimistic. A few delegates were embarrassed by the lack of voting instructions from their governments. Martin intervened with the telephone company to get top priorities for the Latin-American embassies. As the Council meeting went on and on into late afternoon, delegates kept darting to the telephones outside, then back to their seats. Emilio Sarmiento Carruncho of Bolivia had been under strict instructions from his government to boycott the OAS for reasons having nothing to do with Cuba, but rising from a neighborhood dispute. When at last he got through to La Paz, after hours of waiting, the line was so bad he could hear nothing but a distant shouting overpowered by static. Emilio Oribe of Uruguay also failed to receive instructions. At 4:45 P.M. the Council voted. Bolivia's Ambassador Sarmiento decided this was no time to hang back. After abstaining on a single paragraph, he shouted "Sí" to the resolution as a whole. That made the vote 19 to 0, Uruguay alone abstaining. Sarmiento's courage in assuming personal responsibility won Rusk's admiration.

At 9:34 that evening, the Secretary of State sent instructions to Ben Stephansky, United States Ambassador in La Paz, urging that he pass on to the Bolivian President, Washington's gratification "that Bolivia should have put aside a national grievance and taken her place in the Council of the OAS to work collectively with her sister republics in meeting the common danger." Rusk made special mention of Ambassador Sarmiento's "courageous stand."

In New York, Adlai Stevenson was delivering his opening speech in the Security Council when Harlan Cleveland, then Assistant Secretary of State for International Organization Affairs, gave him a note about the unanimous OAS vote. Elated at the outcome, Stevenson promptly read the OAS resolution into the record of the Security Council. There is reason to think that Moscow was staggered by the show of inter-American solidarity and the solid support of the sometimes quarrelsome NATO countries. It left the Russians with no immediate hope of splitting the Western camp. New tactics would have to be devised for manipulating the genuine world-wide fear of imminent war to their own advantage. But that would take time, and more than one false start. Stevenson put the facts of the Soviet arms build-up before the Security Council:

The American republics have lived with dictators before. If this were his only fault, they could live with Dr. Castro. . . . The crucial fact is that Cuba has given the Soviet Union a bridgehead and a staging area in this hemisphere, that it has invited an extra-continental, anti-democratic, expansionist power into the bosom of the American family, that it has made itself an accomplice in the Communist enterprise of world dominion. . . .

In our passion for peace, we have foreborne greatly. But there must be limits to forebearance, if forebearance is not to become the diagram for the destruction of this organization. Dr. Castro transformed Cuba into a totalitarian dictatorship, with impunity; he extinguished the rights of political freedom, with impunity; he aligned himself with the Soviet bloc, with impunity; he accepted defensive weapons from the Soviet Union, with impunity; he welcomed thousands of [foreign] Communists into Cuba, with impunity. But, when with cold deliberation he turns his country over to the Soviet Union for a long-range missile launching base, and thus carries the Soviet program for aggression into the heart of the Americas, the day of forebearance is past.

Zorin, in turn, accused the United States of threatening world war, putting "millions upon millions of human lives" at stake. He rejected "false accusations" that the Soviet Union had "set up offensive armaments in Cuba." Then he produced a draft resolution of his own, which would have the Security Council condemn "the actions of the government of the United States of America aimed at violating the United Nations Charter and at increasing the threat of war." The Cuban representative, Mario Garcia Inchaustegui, denounced the United States, as expected, calling the quarantine a criminal act. Swept along on a torrent of emotional words, he announced that Cuba would never accept any U.N. observers or inspectors on her soil. This outburst cut the ground from under Zorin, who had made a great point of stressing that the Soviet Union would not object to U.N. observers verifying the liquidation of "all foreign bases on foreign territory." (The Cuban delegate evidently said more than he was authorized to say. A week later Castro recalled him to Havana.)

That night the U. S. delegation, after counting noses around the table, informed Washington that it was sure of seven votes, at least, in the eleven-nation Security Council. The African and Asian delegations, for the most part, were not condemning the United States or the Soviet Union. Their fear of war led them to request that U Thant stand between the superpowers, using his influence to keep the tense situation under control. Some of the Afro-Asian delegates clung to the tattered belief that when the big powers start throwing rocks at one another the right posture for the little fellows is to pretend they did not happen to see who threw the first rock. True to this doctrine, Ghana's Alex Quaison-Sackey delivered himself of the opinion that the United States

and the Soviet Union were equally "rascals." Another
African delegate buttonholed an American to announce that his government fully approved the Kennedy decision, but did not dare say so in public. The
Russians, well aware that fear was their best ally,
made certain that the inherent dangers were widely
advertised. Mikhail Polonik, Press Officer to the
Soviet delegation, was particularly assiduous in playing on the fears of other delegations. At nine o'clock
on Tuesday night, he met Ernest G. Wiener, an information officer with the U. S. delegation. Polonik,
in a state of near-explosive tension, told Wiener that
the United States was clearly forcing the Soviet Union to the brink of war. "This could well be our last
conversation," Polonik announced. "New York will be
blown up tomorrow by Soviet nuclear weapons."
He added that the test would come Wednesday when
*Poltava*, the first of the Soviet ships bound for Cuba,
was scheduled to arrive. What would the United
States do about it? Wiener replied that if *Poltava*
tried to pass through the blockade she would necessarily be challenged.

"What do you expect us to do then?" the Russian
asked.

"It's up to you," Wiener said.

In Washington the same evening, at a Soviet Embassy reception, Lieutenant General Vladimir A. Dubovik spread the word that Soviet ship captains heading for Cuba were under orders to defy the blockade. "I fought in three wars already," the Soviet
general said, "and I am looking forward to fighting
in the next. We Russians are ready to defend ourselves against all acts of aggression, against ourselves
or any of our allies. Our ships will sail through. And
if it is decreed that those men must die, then they
will obey their orders and stay on course, or be sunk."
Dubovik's outburst was treated by some guests as a
heavy-handed Muscovite joke. But the general, obviously in earnest, wiped his perspiring hands on a

blue workingman's handkerchief and refused to be silenced. Ambassador Dobrynin, appearing late at the caviar and vodka party, would not refute Dubovik's statement. "He is a military man; I am not," Dobrynin told his startled foreign guests. "He is the one who knows what the Navy is going to do, not I."

Throughout Monday and much of Tuesday a task force of young lawyers had been at work drafting the blockade proclamation. The central figures were Deputy Attorney General Nicholas Katzenbach; John McNaughton, general counsel of the Defense Department; Adam Yarmolinsky, McNamara's special assistant; Ben Foreman of the Justice Department, and Abram Chayes of State. All were Ivy League law school graduates in their early forties. All had known one another as students. Chayes and Yarmolinsky, for example, had been classmates at Harvard College. When Chayes became editor of the *Harvard Law Review*, Yarmolinsky edited the *Yale Law Review*. Foreman, McNaughton and Chayes had worked on the same *Law Review* at Harvard. All four had known Nick Katzenbach for years.

They made short work of the proclamation, titled "Interdiction of Offensive Weapons to Cuba." It had to be ready on Tuesday afternoon and it was. The President was fully prepared to act alone if necessary. But he understood the importance of holding back the proclamation until the OAS had voted. It was, therefore, not until seven o'clock that the President signed the proclamation, basing the blockade squarely on the unanimous OAS vote invoking Articles 6 and 8 of the Rio Treaty of Reciprocal Assistance. Until the last moment, the drafters had left a blank in the list of contraband materials, to include petroleum if necessary. The President decided, however, to reserve that restriction for the future. The only materials prohibited were:

Surface-to-air missiles; bomber aircraft; bombs, air-to-surface rockets and guided missiles; warheads for any of the above weapons; mechanical or electronic equipment to support or operate the above items; and any other class of material hereafter designated by the Secretary of Defense for the purpose of effectuating this proclamation.

Mrs. Lincoln carried the customary tray of pens into the Cabinet Room so the President could use a separate pen for each letter of his name, then hand them round as souvenirs. The President vetoed that idea as wholly inappropriate to the occasion. He signed the proclamation with a single pen, then flipped it into his breast pocket. "This one," he said, "I'm going to keep." The blockade would go into effect Wednesday morning, at ten o'clock eastern time, and until the Russians had shown their hand a great question mark would hang over the whole undertaking. Thanking the drafters of the proclamation, Kennedy said: "We'll all be a lot wiser tomorrow."

There were other loopholes to be closed before the President could be sure that no nuclear warheads would reach Cuba, if they had not already been delivered. The Russians presumably might try to fly them in, and a single Ilyushin could carry enough warheads to arm every missile in Cuba with a deadly nuclear tip. The State Department sent instructions to the American ambassadors in Jamaica and Trinidad, Guinea, and Senegal, asking each to intercede with his host government. Their instructions were to persuade the host governments, where possible, that all Soviet-bloc planes bound for Cuba should be denied landing rights. As a fallback position, if the governments should balk at so sweeping a demand, the ambassadors were instructed to urge the denial of flights carrying military equipment of any kind. Each was instructed to stress that compliance would be deemed a positive demonstration of friendship for the United States and a decisive step toward the preservation of peace.

William Attwood, the Ambassador to Guinea, and Philip M. Kaiser, the Ambassador to Senegal, had the crucially important assignments. Conakry and Dakar were the only practical refueling stops in Africa for Soviet planes en route to Cuba across the South Atlantic. Neither Ambassador was a career diplomat. Attwood had been a newspaperman and magazine editor; Kaiser had been Assistant Secretary of Labor in the Truman Administration and a professor at American University. Attwood knew, when he went to see Guinea's President Sekou Touré, that the Russians the month before had requested landing rights in Conakry for a once-a-week flight from Moscow to Havana. He reckoned the Russians at that moment would be pressing Touré hard for approval. This surmise Touré promptly confirmed. But, the Guinean President explained, as the leader of a sincerely nonaligned nation he could not in good conscience assist anyone in setting up a military base on foreign soil. In short he would refuse the Russian request for landing rights. Touré added that, while he disapproved of what the Soviets were doing in Cuba, he thought it was equally wrong of the Americans to keep their Guantánamo base on Cuban soil. Hence he would refuse to co-operate with the United States in building up Guantánamo. Attwood saw no reason to challenge this rationale. His mission was swiftly accomplished.*

In Dakar, Ambassador Kaiser had fixed an appointment with President Leopold Senghor for 4 P.M., October 23, in behalf of Senator Allen J. Ellender of Louisiana, then on a flying inspection tour of Africa. When the Washington cable arrived, Kaiser asked to see Senghor alone fifteen minutes in advance of Sena-

---

* Touré's assessment of Castro was that, though a genuine neutralist, he had been taken over by the Communists because he lacked "ideological experience" and "intellectual formation." Touré, schooled in Marxism, explained that he would not let this happen in Guinea.

tor Ellender. Kaiser explained what President Kennedy was trying to accomplish in asking that Senegal deny the Russians the use of Dakar airport. Senghor (a distinguished African poet as well as politician) quickly perceived the danger. *"Cela, c'est très grave,"* he said. He promised to refuse if the Russians asked to land at Dakar, citing his attachment to the principles of nonalignment. There is reason to believe that the French Ambassador in Dakar, instructed from Paris to help in any way he could following the de Gaulle interview with Acheson, put in an additional persuasive word with Senghor. Kaiser and Attwood, the amateur diplomats, had closed the African loophole with professional ease.

At the Pentagon that evening. McNamara announced that the latest U-2 photographs showed work going ahead on the Cuban missile sites and twenty-five Soviet ships on the way, their course unchanged in the past twenty-four hours. Under authority granted to the President by Congress, McNamara also ordered the duty tours of all Navy and Marine Corps men extended until further notice.

Sir David and Lady Ormsby Gore had received a pre-crisis invitation to join the Kennedys that evening for a private dinner-dance. The dance, of course, had been canceled. But Mrs. Kennedy invited the Ormsby Gores to bring to dinner some Embassy guests who had arrived from New York too late to be forewarned of the cancellation. The British Ambassador found the President in no mood for social chatter. The two went off together for a talk about the day's events and what the morrow might bring. Sir David was worried about the skeptical British press reaction. Even the President's friend, Hugh Gaitskell, leader of the Labour Opposition, had talked of "so-called missiles" in Cuba. The Ambassador felt it was most important that the missile-site photographs be published, especially those that would most readily persuade laymen that the Soviet missiles were indeed being installed. The President sent for the photographs and together the two re-examined them closely. Ormsby Gore's plea, rein-forcing the direct appeal of Ambassador Bruce in London, helped the President decide to publish the pictures next day. They also discussed Zorin's state-ment in the Security Council. The Russian's denial that the missiles in Cuba were offensive seemed, they agreed, to turn on intent. This added to the Ambas-sador's uneasy feeling that British opinion must somehow be persuaded that the missiles crisis was the real thing, not something trumped up by the President for vote-getting purposes.

At that point, Robert Kennedy walked into the room. He had just seen Dobrynin (the reason the Soviet Ambassador was late for his military attaché's party). It had, by Robert Kennedy's account, been a fruitless encounter. The President's brother reminded Dobrynin of his own past assurances that there were no offensive missiles in Cuba. Dobrynin acknowl-edged them, saying he had in mind a specific as-surance that the missiles in Cuba were "not capable of reaching the United States." Somewhat bitterly, the Attorney General pointed out that on the strength of these false and hypocritical assurances the Presi-dent had told the American people there was no dan-ger from Cuba. We are in for a difficult time, he said to Dobrynin. Dobrynin stolidly kept repeating that so far as he knew there were no Soviet missiles in Cuba with sufficient range to reach the United States. If the United States possessed contrary evidence, he asked, why had the President not mentioned it to Gromyko? The Attorney General replied that Gro-myko certainly knew the truth and that the President had been so shocked by his lying that any effort at intelligent conversation was ruled out. Dobrynin said he too had talked with Gromyko and he was abso-lutely certain that the Soviet Foreign Minister had no knowledge of offensive missiles in Cuba.

The President listened carefully. He appeared slim, handsome, well tailored as ever. But, in the Ambassador's view, Kennedy was anything but cool or calm at the prospect of pushing the world to the brink of nuclear war. The inner tension showed in other ways. He talked at a tremendous pace, in machine-gun bursts. And his eyes were screwed tight as if to shut out the vision of a world in ruins.

*I think your attention might well be directed
to the burglar, rather than to those who caught
the burglar.*
—JOHN F. KENNEDY to Earl Russell, October
26, 1962

AT TEN O'CLOCK, the blockade line was drawn. Nineteen ships of the United States Second Fleet under
its new commander, Vice Admiral Alfred Gustave
Ward, took up stations in a great arc extending 500
miles out to sea from Cape Maysi, Cuba's eastern-
most tip. The line had been drawn four days earlier
with a pair of dividers on a chart of the Caribbean
selling at the Navy Hydrographic Office for $1.20. In
setting the radius at 500 miles, the Navy planners had
two purposes in mind. First, that the line of ships
should be beyond the operating range of MIG fighters based in Cuba. Second, that its distance from
Cuban ports would allow plenty of time for Washington to decide whether any particular ship should
be boarded and searched. Admiral Ward, known to
his Annapolis classmates as Corky, was to have assumed his Second Fleet command in January 1963.
But the Chief of Naval Operations, Admiral Anderson, had decided not to wait so long. On October 12,
through Vice Admiral William R. Smedberg III,
Chief of the Bureau of Personnel, Ward received orders to turn over his own Amphibious Forces, Atlantic
Fleet, command immediately to Vice Admiral Horacio Rivero. Smedberg offered Ward no explanation,
except that Admiral Anderson wanted him on board

the Second Fleet flagship *Newport News* "if something should happen."

The change-of-command ceremony took place in Norfolk, Virginia, on Saturday morning, October 20. All the naval traditions were observed except one. The principal speaker, Admiral Robert L. Dennison, Commander-in-Chief of all Atlantic Forces, did not appear. Dennison had sent word that he was unavoidably detained at his own Atlantic Fleet headquarters one mile away.

Admiral Ward was still shaking hands with guests, following the change-of-command ceremony, when an aide told him a high-priority message was waiting. He found a dispatch from Admiral Dennison, directing him to send six destroyers and two oilers to the Southern Operating Area no later than Sunday, October 21. It was a puzzling order. Except in wartime or in extreme emergency the Navy never sends ships to sea on Sunday. Ward immediately telephoned Dennison. "I have been reading some traffic. Is there anything I should know?" he asked. "There sure is," Dennison replied. "I was waiting for your change-of-command ceremony to end before calling you. Can you come over right now?" That afternoon Ward and Dennison flew to Washington together. There, Admiral Anderson told Ward the President had ordered a blockade of Cuba and that he would be in command. Ward's job was to close off all five navigable channels through which ships from the mid-Atlantic could approach Cuba. He decided to station thirteen destroyers on the forward line, beyond them two cruisers—his flagship *Newport News* and the guided missile cruiser *Canberra,* each of the cruisers to be flanked by two additional destroyers. That made nineteen ships in all, operating as Task Force 136.

Flying back to Norfolk toward midnight on Saturday, Dennison and Ward considered some practical problems. Several of the Norfolk-based destroyers had just returned from service with the Sixth Fleet in the Mediterranean. Many of the crewmen were on leave. How could they be rounded up without violating secrecy? The Admirals decided to call the destroyer captains to Norfolk early Monday morning, October 22, to let them round up those of their men who were in the area, and then to fill out their complements from other ships in drydock.

On Monday afternoon, even as Washington waited feverishly for the President's announcement, the Task Force was on its way, flank speed 27 knots, in Cruise Condition 3—no lights, limited radio communication, secondary batteries manned. As the ships rounded Cape Hatteras, heading for their assigned stations northeast of the Bahamas, the sky was clear and a stiff breeze blowing.

At that hour some twenty-five Soviet ships were strung out across the Atlantic, bound for Cuba. Navy reconnaissance planes had them all spotted, making careful note of those that carried deck cargo, particularly ships built in Japan for the Soviet lumber trade, with extra-large hatches wide enough to accommodate intermediate-range missiles below decks. The position, speed and direction of each Soviet vessel had been carefully plotted. There was reason to expect the first interception in just a few hours.

From Moscow that morning came word that the Soviet Government had sent back to the American Embassy a copy of the President's quarantine proclamation, calling it unacceptable. There was a flurry of excitement when the news agencies rang their bulletin bells by way of alerting editors to a report that Nikita Khrushchev had called for a summit conference. This turned out to be Moscow's reply to a peace appeal from Earl Russell, sent to President Kennedy as well as Khrushchev. "The question of war and peace is so vital," Khrushchev wrote, "that we consider useful a top-level meeting in order to discuss all the problems which have arisen, to do everything to remove the danger of unleashing a thermo-nuclear war. As long as rocket nuclear weapons are not put into play, it is still possible to avert war."

Washington officials, scanning the eastern horizon for some sign of Soviet intentions concerning the blockade, paid more attention to Khrushchev's warning that "if the United States Government carries out the program of piratical actions outlined by it, we shall have to resort to means of defense against the aggressor to defend our rights."

The President brushed aside Earl Russell's message, but on October 26 the philosopher-mathematician-turned-peace-crusader—who once had advocated bombing Russia to force upon her America's plan for control of nuclear energy—received this brief reply:

I am in receipt of your telegram. We are currently discussing the matter in the United Nations. While your messages are critical of the United States, they make no mention of your concern for the introduction of secret Soviet missiles into Cuba. I think your attention might well be directed to the burglars rather than to those who have caught the burglars.

JOHN F. KENNEDY

American embassies round the world had been busy overnight, sounding public opinion. From Tokyo, Ambassador Edwin O. Reischauer reported a feeling among non-Communists that the President's action was "understandable but regrettable." Many Japanese were terrified that war was about to envelop the world, a fear the left-wing forces were skillfully manipulating. In New Delhi, Bombay, and Calcutta, Indian newspapers were generally critical. They accused the United States of violating international law by the blockade of Cuba, warned of possible repercussions in Berlin or Vietnam. Some Indian editors suggested that the Soviet Union might have been justified in establishing Cuban missile bases. After all, they said, the United States had surrounded the

Soviet Union with its own bases. From Paris, Ambassador Bohlen reported that the dominant French attitude, taking its cue from President de Gaulle, was one of "solidarity, understanding and sympathy." At a diplomatic reception a neutral statesman had conspicuously summoned the American minister, Cecil Lyon, to underline his country's sympathy for the United States. From London, Ambassador Bruce reported the nuclear disarmament campaigners were raising a storm. They argued that the President should have taken his case against the Russians to the United Nations before imposing the blockade. Many people in Britain, nuclear disarmers or not, were prepared to believe the worst of President Kennedy: among them Dr. Stephen Thomas Ward, a West End osteopath with a flair for collecting pretty girls to share with his rich friends and an unfulfilled yearning to be counted a very important person. Ward had befriended Captain Eugene Ivanov, naval attaché at the Soviet Embassy, introducing the Russian to a redhaired party girl named Christine Keeler. The world was to hear a great deal about the Ward-Keeler-Ivanov triangle soon after the missiles crisis. But not until a Minister of his own Cabinet had been exposed as a liar did Prime Minister Macmillan tell the House of Commons about the bizarre campaign of Ward and Ivanov to change the course of history.

It started on the day the blockade went into effect, October 24. Ivanov and Ward met for lunch that day and the Russian did most of the talking. Ivanov told Ward that the Americans had created a dangerous situation; they were on a collision course with the Russians and neither side could afford to lose face by seeking a compromise. The British alone could save world peace by calling an immediate summit conference in London. There would be great credit for Britain, Ivanov added, in demonstrating that she was not merely a pawn of Washington but a power capable of independent action for peace.

Ivanov sought to impress Ward with his Kremlin connections. He said he could guarantee Khrushchev's acceptance of a British invitation to immediate summit talks, adding that Khrushchev was prepared to turn back all ships carrying arms to Cuba and to discuss the removal of his missiles already installed. Evidently flattered by Ivanov's confidences, Ward agreed to spread the message among his influential friends.

Prime Minister Macmillan gave the Commons his own account of this episode on June 17, 1963, at the height of another crisis—the domestic crisis over his Secretary of State for War, John Profumo, who twelve days earlier had confessed he lied to the House about his relationship with Christine Keeler.

I confess the last few days have not been agreeable to me [Macmillan said]. But I must say . . . that the week of the Cuban crisis—and I have been through some in peace and war—was the week of most strain I can ever remember in my life. It then seemed to many of us . . . that in the struggle of wills between the Soviet Union and the Western powers, primarily the United States, the world might be coming to the brink of war. During that week, as the pressures developed and built up to the climax on Friday and Saturday, the strain was certainly very great.

Naturally the same was true of the Soviet Government, who were doing all they could to further their policy and weaken the resolution of the West. Part of this Soviet activity was public; for example, the statement issued by the Soviet Government on 23rd October; some of which was private.

Ivanov, with the assistance of Mr. Ward, was perhaps rather more persistent than most. But he was not the only one trying to bring this pressure to shake us and, by us, to bring what pressure we could to bear on the United States.

On 24th October, Ward telephoned the Resident Clerk at the Foreign Office and gave him an account of a conversation he had just had with Ivanov, this to be passed on to Sir Harold Caccia [then Permanent Under Secretary at the Foreign Office].

Ivanov had told him, Ward said, that the Americans had created a situation in which there was no opportunity for either Americans or Russians to compromise and that the Soviet Government looked to the United Kingdom as their one hope of conciliation.

In Washington, the Executive Committee spent the morning discussing the first interception, expected before the day was out. To keep abreast of work on the Soviet missile sites, which was going ahead with astonishing speed, the President authorized special low-level reconnaissance flights by Navy P8U pilots, operating in groups of four to eight planes. Kennedy took a few minutes from his preoccupation with what was to come to thank Latin America for its resounding approval of the blockade in the Organization of American States the previous day. To each of the Latin Chiefs of State, except the abstaining junta in Uruguay, he sent this message:

By your swift and decisive action we have shown the world and particularly the Soviet Union that we stand united in our determination to defend the integrity of the hemisphere and the principles on which our regional system is based.

At 1 P.M. the Administration released for publication in the newspapers and on television fourteen aerial photographs of the missile sites under construction, the original evidence that had prompted the crisis. The President's personal inclination had been not to publish the photographs. But Pierre Salinger and Donald Wilson had argued long and hard that in the absence of published proof the United States could scarcely hope to rally support round the world. Both the American Ambassador in London, David Bruce, and the British Ambassador in Washington, David Ormsby Gore, agreed with this reckoning. It was thanks to their intervention that William Clark, then public affairs officer of the American Embassy in London, had received telephone authorization from Washington to distribute prints of the aerial photographs to the British press and television earlier that day. "It was," Salinger recalls, "the best thing that ever happened. Those pictures played a major role in persuading foreign opinion that the President was justified in taking action." Eventually, the United States Information Agency distributed some 50,000 prints through its posts round the world.

In New York the United Nations Security Council had been meeting since nine o'clock that morning. The nonaligned delegations seemed frightened and wobbly. The Malaysian Ambassador confided that a great number of Africans and Asians felt the United States was in the wrong. Alex Quaison-Sackey of Ghana, for example, took the position that the blockade was unjustified. He contended the United States ought to be satisfied with the assurances already given by the Soviet Union and Cuba that the missiles were defensive in nature. Any state, Quaison-Sackey argued, has the right to take measures to preserve its own security. But its actions must be accompanied by incontrovertible proof that a real threat exists. He doubted that such proof of "Cuba's offensive designs" had been supplied to the Council. This total misreading of the facts already presented bearing on the Soviet Union's direct responsibility for the planting of ballistic missiles in Cuba prevailed among many of the *Asafs* (State Department shorthand for the Asian-African delegations). First McCloy and then Ambassador Stevenson met privately with selected groups of African and Asian ambassadors in hopes they could be persuaded to a more realistic view. Stevenson told them he saw no way to deal with their concern over a clash at sea other than that they should let the Russians know how they felt. The pressure of Afro-Asian opinion, he suggested, might help the Kremlin to decide against challenging the blockade. The Acting Secretary General, U Thant, well aware of the feeling among nonaligned delegations that the United Nations must try to draw the nuclear superpowers apart, made his move at 2 P.M.

He sent identical letters to Kennedy and Khrushchev urging suspension of the blockade and of further arms shipments to Cuba for two or three weeks.

I have been asked by the permanent representatives of a large number of member governments [U Thant wrote to both leaders] . . . to address an urgent appeal to you in the present critical situation.

These representatives feel that in the interest of international peace and security, all concerned should refrain from any action which may aggravate the situation and bring with it the risk of war. In their view, it is important that time should be given to enable the parties concerned to get together, with a view to resolving the present crisis peacefully and normalizing the situation in the Caribbean.

This involves, on the one hand, the voluntary suspension of all arms shipments to Cuba and also the voluntary suspension of the quarantine measure applied, involving the search of ships bound for Cuba. I believe such voluntary suspension for a period of 2 to 3 weeks will greatly ease the situation and give time to the parties concerned to meet and discuss with a view to finding a peaceful solution of the problem.

In this context I shall gladly make myself available to all parties for whatever services I may be able to perform. I urgently appeal to Your Excellency to give immediate consideration to this message.

U THANT
Acting Secretary General

The President was anything but grateful for this intervention, although he recognized that it could not be brushed aside as he had brushed aside Earl Russell's appeal. To accept would be to pull the plug on the elaborate machinery of diplomatic and military pressure that he had just set in motion. The all-important thing was that Khrushchev should be made to realize how near the abyss his rocket diplomacy had carried the world. If U Thant's negotiations were to fail, once the machinery had been disconnected, it might be impossible to start it running again. Kennedy's decision was to refuse negotiations until the Russians showed some willingness to dismantle and remove their Cuban missile bases. He put off his reply until the following day.

In Moscow on that Wednesday afternoon, Nikita Khrushchev sent for a visiting American businessman who could carry a message back to Washington. The visitor was William Knox, President of Westinghouse International, once a neighbor of Dean Rusk in Scarsdale, New York. Knox's business in the Soviet Union was not with the Kremlin leaders but with Licensintorg, a new state trading organization that wanted advice on international patent procedures. He was just saying good-bye to the head of Licensintorg after a friendly luncheon when summoned to the Kremlin for an unsolicited, wholly unexpected three o'clock appointment with the Chairman of the Soviet Council of Ministers. Khrushchev's motivation, it would seem, was to let Kennedy know through a private channel that he did have missiles in Cuba, something his ambassadors in New York and Washington were still indignantly denying.

Knox arrived fifteen minutes late to find Khrushchev in a state of near-exhaustion. He looked like a man who had not slept all night. For three hours he treated Knox to a succession of threats, complaints and peasant jokes. It was true, he said, the Soviet Union had missiles and attack planes in Cuba; moreover he would use them if need be.

He wanted the President and the American people to know, Khrushchev added, that if the United States Navy tried to stop Soviet ships at sea, his submarines would start sinking American ships. And that would mean a third world war. Khrushchev complained that he could not understand Kennedy. Eisenhower had been troublesome enough, but Eisenhower was a man of his own generation. "How can I deal with a man who is younger than my son?" he asked the astonished Westinghouse man. Then, extending a stubby index finger across the table in Knox's direction, he talked of weapons, offensive and defensive. "If I point a pistol at you like this in order to attack you," Khrushchev said, "the pistol is an offensive weapon. But if I aim to keep you from shooting me, it is defensive, no?"

Knox replied that he was no military man. But he had noticed that Khrushchev's neighbors, the Swedes, had modern antiaircraft guns and interceptor planes but no bombers or missiles capable of attacking the Soviet Union. Surely intent alone, Knox said, did not determine whether a weapon was offensive or defensive. Khrushchev soon changed the subject. Knox left Moscow the next day and delivered the message to Washington.

At 4 P.M. the Pentagon reporters—their thin ranks reinforced during the crisis by dozens of newcomers normally assigned to Capitol Hill, Commerce, Agriculture or Interior—were called into Arthur Sylvester's office. He produced a set of twelve regulations specifying various categories of military information that was not to be made public for the duration of the crisis. It would be considered "contrary to the national interest," for example, for officers of the Defense Department or the armed services to give out details of troop movements, operational plans, intelligence estimates concerning possible targets—in short the kinds of restrictions that are customary in time of war. The Administration had no legislative authority to forbid publication by newspapers, radio or television networks. But the White House appealed for the exercise of discretion by editors and publishers in dealing with national security matters of this kind.

Sylvester then announced that intelligence analysts in the CIA and the Defense Department's own intelligence agency had taken the measure of the current threat. "There are," he said, "eight to ten bases located in areas near the cities of Guanajay, Remedios, San Cristóbal and Sagua la Grande, each base having about four launchers, more or less. Reports from all intelligence sources confirm," Sylvester added, "that at least thirty missiles and more than twenty IL-28 jet light bombers are present in Cuba. This evidence is undeniable. U.S.S.R. personnel numbering at least 5,000 are now in Cuba. The exact number cannot be determined. . . ."

Reporters pressed him to confirm or deny reports already broadcast by the National Broadcasting Company and the American Broadcasting Company to the effect that certain of the Russian ships bound for Cuba had altered course or turned back. "I can't either confirm or deny it," he said. At 5:15 P.M., after further checking, a Defense Department spokesman half-confirmed the report: "Some of the [Soviet] bloc vessels proceeding toward Cuba *appear* to have altered course," he said. "Other vessels are proceeding toward Cuba. No intercepts have yet been necessary."

Inside the Cabinet Room the President and his advisors had been braced for a perilous encounter at sea. "The greatest danger of war as we saw it then," Paul Nitze recalls, "was that we would sink a Russian ship trying to run the blockade. If that happened, it seemed highly doubtful that Khrushchev would hold still without further action."

That afternoon came the first glimmer of hope that Khrushchev might not, after all, challenge the blockade. A dozen of the twenty-five ships, it began to appear, had changed course or stopped. Dean Rusk, sitting at the President's right hand, nudged McGeorge Bundy and said softly: "We're eyeball to eyeball and I think the other fellow just blinked." It was hard to

know what the blink meant. At the Pentagon the reaction was unexpectedly somber. Far from assuming
that the worst might be over, the military chiefs speculated that the twelve ships might have altered course
for a sinister purpose: perhaps they were going to
rendezvous with Soviet submarines, six of which had
been reported in the area, and would then try to force
their way through the line of American ships. With
these uncertainties still to be resolved, the President
determined that Khrushchev must have time to think,
and to transmit instructions in cold blood to his ship
captains at sea. Precipitate action was ruled out. The
President directed McNamara to make certain there
was no shooting. Soviet ships approaching the interception area were to be followed, kept in view, but
not boarded until the Navy received fresh instructions.

To satisfy himself that the Navy understood the
President's instructions, McNamara went to call on Admiral Anderson about ten o'clock that night. The Secretary of Defense had been spending the crisis nights
on a cot in his imposing third-floor office on the Pentagon's E Ring. It is in E Ring, the outermost in a
series of concentric corridors, that the power of decision is concentrated. With his deputy, Roswell Gilpatric, McNamara made his way to the fourth floor
and discovered Anderson in the Navy Flag Plot. This
was the command center of the quarantine operation,
a big room under constant Marine guard, dominated
by vast wall charts of the seven seas.

The encounter started badly. McNamara spotted a
marker showing an American ship off by itself on the
vast ocean, far away from the interception area.
"What's it doing there?" he asked. Anderson did not
answer directly because—as he later explained—too
many others were listening. Eventually he drew Mc-
Namara aside and explained that the lone ship was
sitting on top of a Soviet submarine.* McNamara

* At a Navy League banquet in New York on November
9, 1962, Anderson said: "The presence of many Russian sub-

asked about the first interception: exactly what would the Navy do? Anderson replied there was no need to discuss the issue; the Navy had known all there was to know about running a blockade since the days of John Paul Jones. But McNamara was not to be put off. "We must discuss it," he said; then carefully explained:

The object of the operation was not to shoot Russians but to communicate a political message from President Kennedy to Chairman Khrushchev. The President wanted to avoid pushing Khrushchev to extremes. The blockade must be so conducted as to avoid humiliating the Russians; otherwise Khrushchev might react in a nuclear spasm. By the conventional rules, blockade was an act of war and the first Soviet ship that refused to submit to boarding and search risked being sent to the bottom. But this was a military action with a political objective. Khrushchev must somehow be persuaded to pull back, rather than be goaded into retaliation.

Methodically the Secretary of Defense quizzed the Chief of Operations about details—the kind of details, Navy men insist, that civilians have no business worrying about. No Secretary of Defense had ever spoken that way to a member of the Joint Chiefs of Staff. He asked whether there was a Russian-speaking officer on each blockading destroyer. Anderson confessed he did not know. Then find out, McNamara said. (In fact the Navy had foreseen this need and, among others, had assigned several Annapolis language instructors to blockade duty.) Eyewitnesses to this strange encounter—there were about thirty in the

marines in Caribbean and Atlantic waters provided perhaps the finest opportunity since World War II for U. S. Naval antisubmarine warfare forces to exercise at their trade, to perfect their skills and to manifest their capability to detect and follow submarines of another nation." He might have added that the Navy harried them mercilessly. Each of the six submarines was forced to surface. At no time were weapons fired.

Flag Plot at the time—agree that both men were under great strain—McNamara struggling to hold his temper in check, a hardening glint in his eye; the Admiral red-faced, equally determined not to lose control of himself. Witnesses disagree only about what followed. One group says that Anderson, at a certain point, accused McNamara of "undue interference in naval matters." The Admiral, now Ambassador to Portugal, says this is not his recollection, adding that he was brought up never to say such a thing even if he felt it. At another point, McNamara asked Anderson what he would do if a Soviet ship's captain refused, when challenged, to answer questions about his cargo. One version has it that Anderson at that point picked up a Manual of Naval Regulations, and, waving it in McNamara's face, replied: "It's all in there." To which McNamara is supposed to have retorted: "I don't give a damn what John Paul Jones would have done. I want to know what you are going to do, now." Anderson says he can't remember putting it that way.

The encounter ended abruptly when Anderson said to McNamara: "Now, Mr. Secretary, if you and your deputy will go back to your offices, the Navy will run the blockade." Making no reply, McNamara walked out.*

It was a long worry-filled night for the Under Secretary of State, George Ball. Like McNamara, Ball had received reports of Russian merchantmen moving steadily toward the line of American destroyers. Like McNamara, he felt the situation was far too serious

---

* Admiral Anderson was not reappointed when his two-year term expired in June 1963. Roswell Gilpatric took responsibility for recommending to the President that a new Chief of Naval Operations be appointed because, he said, there could never again exist between Anderson and McNamara the necessary relationship of mutual confidence and loyalty. They had clashed also in the dispute over the TFX fighter, when Anderson testified openly against McNamara's recommendations. To soften the blow, President Kennedy offered Anderson the embassy in Lisbon. After a few days' hesitation, Anderson accepted.

to be left in the hands of the Navy professionals; a single warning shot fired across the bow of a Russian ship might loose the hounds of war. That Wednesday night, alone in his office, Ball talked with Adlai Stevenson by telephone.

"The Secretary General [U Thant] ought to be doing everything possible to avert an encounter between ships at sea in the next twenty-four hours," Ball said to Stevenson. "We need time for the Soviet Union to think things over and for diplomacy to have a chance to work. Why don't you get him to issue an appeal to the Russians to stop their ships for a time? We could have a shooting war by tomorrow afternoon."

Stevenson, in New York, hesitated to disturb Thant's sleep, though he promised to try Thursday morning. Less than satisfied, Ball picked up the direct-line telephone to the White House. It was close to midnight when Ball told Kennedy of his fears that in a matter of minutes or hours, American and Russian ships might be firing at one another. It would be too late then for United Nations intervention. Ball recalls asking the President whether Thant should not be roused from his bed. Perhaps the Secretary General could be persuaded to intervene with the Russians, Ball suggested, "to hold their ships dead in the water until things could be better sorted out." Kennedy agreed that there would be no harm in trying.

Once again Ball telephoned Stevenson in New York, who at last agreed to waken U Thant and put the time-buying proposition to him. All night long Ball waited for word that the Secretary General had in fact intervened with the Russians. No word came.

*Do you, Ambassador Zorin, deny that the
U.S.S.R. has placed and is placing medium-
and intermediate-range missiles and sites in
Cuba. Yes or no? Don't wait for the transla-
tion, yes or no?*
—ADLAI STEVENSON to Soviet Ambassador
Valerian Zorin in the United Nations Security
Council, October 25, 1962

WALTER LIPPMANN (Harvard, 1910) watched the crisis
unfold, oppressed by an old man's tragic sense of
having been through it all before. In his newspaper
column that morning, Lippmann appealed unmistakably to the young President (Harvard, 1940) not to
repeat the mistakes of Woodrow Wilson and Franklin Roosevelt in suspending diplomatic action as the
guns were about to speak. Lippmann was particularly
troubled by Kennedy's demand that the Russians must
dismantle and remove the missiles from Cuba.

How this is to be done is a very great question
[Lippmann wrote], even supposing that there is no
shooting conflict at sea. And it is here, I believe, that
diplomacy must not abdicate.

There are three ways to get rid of the missiles already in Cuba. One is to invade and occupy Cuba.
The second way is to institute a total blockade, particularly of oil shipments, which would in a few
months ruin the Cuban economy. The third way is to
try, I repeat, to try to negotiate a face-saving agreement.

I hasten to say at once that I am not talking about,
and do not believe in, a "Cuba-Berlin" horse trade.

Cuba and Berlin are wholly different cases. Berlin is
not an American missile base. It is not a base for any
kind of offensive, as Cuba is by way of becoming.

The only place that is truly comparable with Cuba
is Turkey. This is the only place where there are
strategic weapons right on the frontier of the Soviet
Union. . . .

There is another important similarity between
Cuba and Turkey. The Soviet missile base in Cuba,
like the U.S.-NATO base in Turkey, is of little military value. The Soviet military base in Cuba is de-
fenseless and the base in Turkey is all but obsolete.
The two bases could be dismantled without altering
the world balance of power.

The President certainly read Lippmann's face-saving proposal in the Washington *Post*. So also did the
Soviet Ambassador. There is reason to think that
Dobrynin saw in it a trial balloon floated by the
White House. The Russians evidently reasoned that if
Walter Lippmann could advocate bartering American
missile bases in Turkey for Soviet missile bases in
Cuba, then surely the President must have given serious thought to such an exchange. It was a faulty
assumption, of which more was to be heard before
long.

While the Lippmann column was providing break-
fast-table conversation in Washington, the first interception of a Soviet ship took place at sea. At eight
o'clock, twenty-two hours after the quarantine order had gone into effect, the Soviet tanker *Bucharest*
was allowed to pass through the line of warships on
her way to Cuba, after identifying herself, by radio,
and declaring she carried nothing but petroleum. At
8:35 A.M. the East German passenger ship *Voelkerfreund*, with twenty students bound for Havana, also
cleared the screen of blockading destroyers. Again
there was no boarding, in strict obedience to the
President's order that sufficient time be allowed for
each ship's captain to receive instructions from Moscow before a confrontation took place.

Early that morning, Thomas L. Hughes, then deputy director of State Department intelligence, flew to
New York for the first of two Congressional briefings.
A second group of Midwestern Congressmen was
waiting to hear him in Chicago. Governor Rockefeller
of New York and New Jersey's Governor Richard J.
Hughes joined the group at the Federal Court House
in Foley Square along with Congressmen of both
parties from other Northeastern states. Tom Hughes
gave them the latest intelligence estimates, pointing
out details of the missile sites under construction with
the help of before-and-after photographs.

He told them about the *Bucharest* interception. Two
hours of questioning followed, some of it sharply political questioning. The election, after all, was exactly eleven days in the future.

Within minutes, first word that the *Bucharest* had
passed through the blockade without interference
from the U. S. Navy was announced, not by the Pentagon—as Kennedy had directed—but by one of the
Congressmen walking out of the New York briefing.
The radio-television networks and the wire services
quoted Representative James Van Zandt, Republican
of Pennsylvania. Van Zandt was in the final days
of his unsuccessful campaign to unseat Senator
Joseph C. Clark, a Democrat. The President heard
about Van Zandt's announcement from Salinger at
that morning's Executive Committee meeting. He was
furious.

Of all this Tom Hughes knew next to nothing until
he reached Idlewild Airport about noon, to catch the
plane for his second briefing of the day in Chicago.
An agitated public-address announcer was paging
him tirelessly: "The President is calling American passenger Hughes. . . . The President is calling American
passenger Hughes. . . ." At the American Airlines
check-in counter, Hughes discovered he had become
a local celebrity. But the Washington line had gone
dead. He dashed to the nearest phone booth, put in

a dime and told the operator the President had been
trying to reach him. The lady, a member in good
standing of the "Don't kid me, mister" sisterhood,
was not impressed.

"Who?" she inquired, somewhat sourly.

"The President of the United States, President Kennedy," Hughes explained.

The lady was not persuaded. Hughes pleaded, told
her his name and his job. The Chicago plane was
about to leave when the operator finally raised Washington. Mrs. Evelyn Lincoln, the President's secretary, assured her it was no hoax. The President picked
up the phone, still seething over Van Zandt's disclosure.

"What the hell is going on up there?" he asked.
"These briefings were set up to take the Congressmen
into our confidence. We haven't even decided what
to do about the tanker." *

Hughes explained and the President's anger sub-
sided. The Pentagon had put out much the same
story fifteen minutes after Van Zandt. Hughes flew
off to Chicago for another round of questions from
the Midwestern Congressmen. And the President returned to his seat in the Executive Committee. Although work on the missile sites was going ahead,
the Committee heard one hopeful piece of information that morning. Navy reconnaissance confirmed
overnight the report that twelve of the twenty-five
Soviet vessels on the way to Cuba had turned back.
Presumably the twelve that received orders not to
risk running the blockade carried incriminating cargoes.

At 11:50 A.M. Arthur Sylvester made the announcement at the Pentagon. "It now appears," he said, "that
at least a dozen Soviet vessels have turned back
because—according to the best of our information—

---

* The Navy was under orders to follow the ships it passed
through the blockade, so they could again be intercepted if
the situation were to change abruptly.

they might have been carrying offensive materials."

It looked like a turning point. To damp down any premature jubilation, Dean Rusk called in the regular State Department reporters for a "deep background" briefing. The source was not to be identified. "I hope you don't create a temporary feeling of euphoria," he told them. "The situation is still extremely grave. We do not at the present time see exactly where it is going to come out. So much depends on the reaction of the other side. The key issue is the presence of these weapons in Cuba. The object is to get them out of there, without war, if possible."

A reporter asked the Secretary of State why the President had chosen to confront the Soviet Union directly, instead of holding Castro responsible for the threat to peace. Rusk replied: "These were Soviet weapons. Removing the weapons had to be a Soviet action. I think if you wanted to put a fig leaf on this situation [by pretending that Castro, not Khrushchev, was responsible] it would have lasted about five minutes. Then we would have looked foolish. The issue is not Castro. It's offensive Soviet weapons."

The euphoria Rusk warned against broke surface quickly enough in unexpected places. The American Embassy in Beirut reported scenes of public jubilation, inspired by reports that the Russian ships had turned around. From Manila, the embassy reported: "Tension much relieved."

Moscow had not yet abandoned Rusk's fig leaf. *Pravda* and *Izvestia* published for the first time that day the three-day-old United States accusation that the Soviet Union had installed offensive missiles in Cuba, and alongside it a half-page summary of Zorin's U.N. speech, denying the charge and denouncing the quarantine as a "new and extremely dangerous act of aggression" by the United States. All a Russian reader could have gleaned from this was that the mighty United States had declared war on little Cuba, with the Soviet Union in the role of innocent bystander. *Pravda*, that morning, published on its front page a "Letter to America" from the young poet Yevgeni Yevtushenko. It was a kind of *Pravda* editorial in verse, telephoned from Havana the night before:

America, I'm writing to you from Cuba,
Where the crags and the cheekbones
Of rigid sentries shine anxiously tonight
In the gusting storm.

Their shadows are huge as Gulliver.
Ministers and doctors, wasting no words,
Exchange their jackets and *guayaberas* *
For uniforms smelling bitterly of campfires.

A tobacconist, carrying a revolver, prepares to leave
        for the harbor,
A shoemaker cleans an old machine gun,
A showgirl from a cabaret, wearing army boots,
Goes along with a carpenter to stand guard.

Abandoning their brushes and their arguments,
Both the realist and the nonobjective painter
Hurry down to the quay in the rain,
Sternly testing their machine guns.

America, I'll ask you in Russian:
Isn't it shameful that out of bigotry
You force them to take up arms
And then accuse them of having done so?!

In the fight against malodorous calumny,
In exhausting struggle against the blockade,
They treat you, America,
In more high-minded, nobler fashion.

They grieve for your children and your grandchildren,
And, at church, sorrowing for your soul,
Four Negro women pray God
To stop you, America.

* A loose-fitting field-jacket of the kind Castro often wears.

I heard Fidel speak. He made his survey
At once like a doctor and a prosecutor.
In his speech, there was not a trace of animosity,
Only sincere bitterness and reproach.

Long since, when young, he ran lightly up the steps,
To the music of birds singing,
He, Fidel, stood before Lincoln's statue,
And looked into his eyes.

Now, speaking of the injustice done,
Clenching his powerful fist,
Fidel looks candidly into Lincoln's eyes;
As for Lincoln, I don't know about Lincoln. . . .

Raising a cry from a lofty platform,
America, how could you permit
This disgracing of freedom,
By unworthy words?

You have offended not only the Cubans
By parading your arrogant fleet;
You have offended divers peoples,
Your own among them.

I know your people. They are kind of heart.
It isn't that I don't care a fig about their fate!
It is painful and terrible for me to see
The vile deeds of a great country.

It grieves me now to be silent for all
Who have forgotten the essence of their sacred rights.
Is it possible, America, that you are degenerating,
Having trampled upon your own majesty?

It isn't a simple matter to recover lost majesty.
You are losing it in a blind game,
And a small, though manly, island
Is becoming a great country!

Havana, October 24

In Prague, beginning at 2:15 P.M. Central European time, some 2,000 demonstrators marched in front of the American Embassy carrying "Hands Off Cuba" placards. The Stars and Stripes was ripped from the flagpole. And some windows were smashed in the United States Consulate. The embassy reported widespread concern among Czechoslovaks over the possibility of war. Inevitably, Prague housewives started a wave of scare-buying. There was enough flour and sugar in the shops to withstand the onslaught. But salt and cooking oil disappeared from the shelves. Remarkably few soldiers showed themselves in the streets, suggesting that military leaves might have been canceled.

The Russian leaders, it soon developed, were no less alarmed than the housewives of Prague. In the words of a British Ambassador: "By Thursday, they were damn scared. They needed something to cover their nakedness—a way out, without humiliation." That day the Soviet chargé d'affaires in London, V. A. Loginov, called on Lord Home, then Foreign Secretary, at his own request. Loginov—so Prime Minister Macmillan later told the House of Commons —"expressed the hope that Her Majesty's Government would do all in its power to avert developments in Cuba which, as he said, could push the world to the brink of a military catastrophe. Mr. Loginov's aim was, apparently, that Her Majesty's Government should bring pressure to bear on the United States Government. Similarly, many members of the Soviet Embassy, not only in London but, I think, elsewhere, were making approaches to various diplomatic missions in London."

Stephen Ward's friend, Captain Ivanov, was among the most active of these emissaries. Kennedy's blockade order had shocked a good many Britons who, like Walter Lippmann, feared the drift to war might prove uncontrollable and felt powerless to stop it. Several impeccably Conservative newspapers had proclaimed their lack of confidence in Kennedy's ability to go to the threshold of nuclear war and then step back. The President had no moral right, some newspapers said, to endanger world peace for the sake of a few real or imaginary missiles in Cuba. Ward, the artist-osteopath with friends or patients in high places, arranged for Ivanov to call on Sir Godfrey Nicholson, Conservative Member of Parliament. Ivanov told the Tory baronet about his plan for Britain to save the peace by a dramatic appeal to both sides for an urgent summit conference, to be held in London. He asked for some indication that the British Government would consider trying to bring about such negotiations. Sir Godfrey made a full report on his conversation with Ivanov to Sir Hugh Stevenson, at the Foreign Office. Later the same afternoon, Ward himself delivered much the same message to Sir Harold Caccia's private secretary.

The pattern of Soviet overtures was interesting: at one level, the official representative of the Soviet Government, Loginov, talking in general terms to Lord Home about the danger of nuclear war and appealing, in a general way, for the British to use their influence with the Americans; at a lower level, Captain Ivanov using the social contacts of Stephen Ward to deliver a more concrete proposal through a back-bench Member of Parliament with good connections. The gambit was clearly intended. Lord Home later observed, to achieve a double purpose: "First, it was to drive a wedge between ourselves and our American allies. Second, it was to test our resolve and to lay a bait to our vanity."

At 2:19 P.M. Washington time, President Kennedy replied to U Thant's message of the previous day, appealing for the Russians to suspend arms shipments to Cuba and for the Americans to call off the quarantine for a period of two or three weeks, so that negotiations could go forward. Kennedy's reply:

Excellency:

I deeply appreciate the spirit which prompted your message of yesterday.

As we made clear in the Security Council, the existing threat was created by the secret introduction of offensive weapons into Cuba, and the answer lies in the removal of such weapons.

In your message and your statement to the Security Council last night, you have made certain suggestions and have invited preliminary talks to determine whether satisfactory arrangements can be assured.

Ambassador Stevenson is prepared to discuss these arrangements with you.

I can assure you of our desire to reach a satisfactory and a peaceful solution of the matter.

                                        JOHN F. KENNEDY

Clearly, the President was keeping the pressure on. The missiles in Cuba would simply have to be removed. Nothing else would do. And until that happened, the blockade must remain in force. There was to be no reliance on Khrushchev's word alone. The United States was willing to talk, so long as Thant understood there could be no limitation of its freedom to act.

Khrushchev's reply the same day was brief and affirmative:

I have received your appeal and carefully studied the proposal it contains. I welcome your initiative. I understand your anxiety over the situation obtaining in the Caribbean, since the Soviet Government also regards the situation as highly dangerous and calling for immediate intervention by the United Nations. I declare that I agree with your proposal, which accords with the interests of peace.

                                        N. S. KHRUSHCHEV

George Ball had waited anxiously all night long and through the morning while U Thant weighed his modest proposal for averting an armed clash at sea. He remembers having "needled Adlai" two or three times by telephone. Each time Stevenson assured the Under Secretary of State that the matter was on the track. Finally, at 2:26 P.M., Thant acted. To Khrushchev, Thant appealed for assurances that Soviet ships on their way to Cuba would keep out of the interception area for a limited time "in order to permit discussion of the modalities of a possible agreement which could settle the problem peacefully in line with the charter of the United Nations." To Kennedy, Thant appealed for specific orders that all United States vessels in the Caribbean should "do everything possible to avoid confrontation with Soviet ships in the next few days in order to minimize the risk of any untoward incident."

The President himself, fully aware of the dangers in an untoward incident, had already done so. Through McNamara he had issued the most explicit instructions to Admiral Anderson. Up to that time there had been no boarding attempt. This was not happenstance but Presidential caution at work.

To sink a Russian ship at that moment, Kennedy believed, would be to drive Khrushchev into a corner, perhaps to force a desperate Soviet response. He felt it was important to establish the principle of the quarantine without humiliating the Russians. After careful discussion of the alternatives between the Pentagon, the White House, and the State Department, the Executive Committee decided that the first ship to be boarded should belong neither to the Soviet Union nor to the Western allies but, preferably, to a neutral nation.

In New York that afternoon, the Security Council met again in an atmosphere of almost unbearable tension. The corridors were filled with talk of imminent war. Ambassadors of the Asian and African nations, for the most part, believed that even the limited quarantine was an extreme remedy. Adlai Stevenson reached back into his treasury of Lincoln stories for a homely answer.

He told the story of a passer-by out in the Lincoln country of Illinois who, when charged by a farmer's ferocious boar, picked up a pitchfork and met the boar head on. The boar died, and the irate farmer asked why he had not used the blunt end of the pitchfork. The man replied: "Why didn't the boar attack me with his blunt end?"

For an instant, Stevenson's Lincoln story relieved the tension. But Valerian Zorin was not amused. The Soviet Ambassador to the United Nations made the mistake of challenging Stevenson to produce hard evidence in proof of his allegation that Moscow had installed long-range missiles in Cuba. Invoking the right of response, Stevenson unveiled the evidence with a fine, dramatic flourish of the kind that his Presidential campaigns so conspicuously lacked.

STEVENSON: Well, let me say something to you, Mr. Ambassador: we do have the evidence. We have it, and it is clear and incontrovertible. And let me say something else: Those weapons must be taken out of Cuba. . . . You, the Soviet Union, have sent these weapons to Cuba. You, the Soviet Union, have created this new danger—not the United States. . . .

Finally, Mr. Zorin, I remind you that the other day you did not deny the existence of these weapons. But today, again if I heard you correctly, you now say that they do not exist, or that we haven't proved they exist.

All right, Sir, let me ask you one simple question. Do you, Ambassador Zorin, deny that the U.S.S.R. has placed and is placing medium- and intermediate-range missiles and sites in Cuba? *Yes* or *no*? Don't wait for the translation, *yes* or *no*?

ZORIN: I am not in an American courtroom, Sir, and therefore I do not wish to answer a question that is put to me in the fashion in which a prosecutor puts questions. In due course, Sir, you will have your answer. *

---

* Stevenson took no pride in having played "Mr. District Attorney" at the height of the missiles crisis. When he visited

STEVENSON: You are in the courtroom of world opinion right now and you can answer *yes* or *no*. You have denied that they exist and I want to know whether I have understood you correctly.

ZORIN: Continue with your statement. You will have your answer in due course.

STEVENSON: I am prepared to wait for my answer until hell freezes over, if that's your decision. And I am also prepared to present the evidence in this room.

With that Stevenson turned to blow-up photographs of the missile sites, standing behind him on a set of shrouded easels. Zorin never did answer the question. He ridiculed the photographic evidence, saying the Soviet Union had no need to station missiles in Cuba. It was a bleak performance and Stevenson had the last word.

"We know the facts, and so do you, Sir, and we are ready to talk about them," Stevenson said. "Our job here is not to score debating points. Our job, Mr. Zorin, is to save the peace. And if you are ready to try, we are."

The Security Council adjourned at 7:25 P.M. so the Secretary General could hold discussions with the Americans, the Russians and the Cubans. It did not meet again until the crisis was past.

---

Moscow the following summer to see the limited nuclear test ban treaty signed, Khrushchev reproached him. "What's happened to you, Stevenson, since you started working for the United States Government?" Khrushchev asked. "We don't like to be interrogated like a criminal in the dock." When Stevenson told the story, a few months before his death, he seemed regretful that the Kremlin leaders no longer considered him "objective."

*If you have not lost your self-control and sensibly conceive what this might lead to, then, Mr. President, we and you ought not now to pull on the ends of the rope in which you have tied the knot of war, because the more we pull, the tighter the knot will be tied.*
—NIKITA KHRUSHCHEV to John F. Kennedy, from an unpublished letter of October 26, 1962

AT PRECISELY seven o'clock that morning the United States destroyer *Joseph P. Kennedy Jr.* hailed the freighter *Marucla* and ran up the international flag hoist "Oscar November." To seafaring men, the flag means: "You should heave to. Stop at once." *Marucla* hove to. She was an American-built Liberty ship, Panamanian-owned though of Lebanese registry, bound for Cuba under Soviet charter from the Baltic port of Riga.

*Marucla* had been sighted at about 10:30 P.M. on Thursday by the United States destroyer *John R. Pierce.* Soon after midnight *Kennedy* joined *Pierce* on patrol, their instructions to stop and board *Marucla* at the first light of day. The rest of the night the two destroyers trailed *Marucla* at a distance of about two miles, waiting for dawn. Both talked with *Marucla*'s skipper by radio. He seemed more than willing to cooperate.

The encounter took place in the open sea, some 180 miles northeast of Nassau. It had been planned with meticulous care by President Kennedy himself. Acting on Llewellyn Thompson's advice that nothing would be gained by a gratuitous affront to Khrushchev, the President had issued detailed instructions: the first boarding and search operation of the Cuban quarantine was to be carried out on a dry cargo ship of neutral registry sailing under Soviet charter. *Marucla* admirably served the President's purpose. He wanted Khrushchev to know that the United States Navy was now exercising the right, claimed in his quarantine proclamation, to stop and search all vessels bound for Cuba, regardless of national registry.

At 7:24 A.M. an unarmed boarding party from both U. S. destroyers, in white service uniform, stood by its whaleboat. At 7:29 the boat was lowered over *Kennedy*'s side. At 7:32 *Marucla* dropped a Jacobs ladder over her side. By 7:50 the boarding party sent back the message: "Party aboard *Marucla*. Cooperation good. No difficulties expected."

The boarding officer, Lieutenant Commander K. C. Reynolds, announced himself to *Marucla*'s master, who raised no objection to the search. After examining the ship's records and the contents of one hold, Reynolds satisfied himself the ship carried no weapons—only sulphur, newsprint rolls, trucks and spare parts. *Marucla* was allowed to sail on.

By the time the news reached Washington, the Executive Committee was meeting again in a mood of collective gloom. True, *Marucla* had quietly submitted to boarding, presumably on instructions from Moscow. But work on the missile sites was going ahead rapidly. The latest aerial photographs left no room for doubt that the Russians were racing to put them into operation. McNamara showed considerable agitation as the talk round the table turned inevitably to the possibility of an air strike. Time was running out. In a matter of hours, the Soviet missiles could be ready to fire. Some said the lesser danger was to knock them out before they could threaten the United States.

Instead the President ordered more low-level reconnaissance flights, one every two hours. He also decided to step up the psychological pressure.

Adlai Stevenson had flown down from New York for the Friday morning session. Kennedy instructed him to make it unmistakably clear, in his private talks with U Thant, that the United States would not be shaken in its determination to get the missiles out of Cuba. There was to be no wobbling. The time had come to turn the screw. At the regular noon briefing, the State Department spokesman, Lincoln White, called attention to a sentence in the President's quarantine speech of Monday night warning the Russians to stop their military build-up. "Should these offensive military preparations continue," Kennedy had said, "thus increasing the threat to the hemisphere, further action will be justified." By underlining this sentence in public, Washington reminded Khrushchev that should the blockade fail to dislodge the missiles, more direct armed action would be ordered. Later in the day Pierre Salinger called a White House news conference to turn the screw once again. He gave the reporters a statement:

The development of ballistic missile sites in Cuba continues at a rapid pace. Through the process of continued surveillance directed by the President, additional evidence has been acquired which clearly reflects that as of Thursday, October 25, definite build-up in these missile sites continued to be made. The activity at these sites apparently is directed at achieving a full operational capability as soon as possible. . . . There is no evidence to date indicating that there is any [Soviet] intention to dismantle or discontinue work on these missile sites. On the contrary, the Soviets are rapidly continuing their construction of missile support and launch facilities, and serious attempts are under way to camouflage their efforts.

All at once, tight-lipped officials turned talkative

and talkative Congressmen turned garrulous. Clement Zablocki, Democrat from Wisconsin, spoke ominously to reporters about a resort to "pinpoint bombing" of the missile bases before long. Admiral Dennison announced that thanks to reinforcements, now in position, Guantánamo could be successfully defended against attack. And Robert Kennedy passed the word to Ambassador Dobrynin that the President could not hold off more than two days longer.

U Thant had appealed to Khrushchev to keep Soviet ships out of the interception area. He also pleaded with Kennedy to "do everything possible to avoid direct confrontation with Soviet ships in the next few days." Both leaders agreed.

Kennedy's reply carried a cautionary postscript:

I must, however, inform you that this is a matter of great urgency, in view of the fact that certain Soviet ships are still proceeding toward Cuba and the interception area. I share your hope that Chairman Khrushchev will also heed your appeal and that we can then proceed urgently to meet the requirements that these offensive missile systems in Cuba be withdrawn in order to end the threat to peace. I must point out to you that work on these systems is still continuing.

There was action to match the talk of a greater crisis ahead. The Army moved antiaircraft missiles into Key West, opposite Cuba. Plans for a series of air attacks on the missile bases, to be followed by an invasion of Cuba, were discussed and refined in the Executive Committee that afternoon. The President authorized Donald Wilson of USIA to print five million leaflets in Spanish. They were to flutter down over Havana, Camaguey, Santa Clara, and Matanzas when and if the attack took place, by way of explaining to Cubans how the United States had been forced to make war.

It was an exhausting day for anyone caught up in the crisis. John Scali, diplomatic correspondent of the American Broadcasting Company, was sitting in his pressroom cubicle at the State Department, gulping down a bologna sandwich, when the telephone rang. It was 1:30 P.M. The caller was a Russian named Alexander S. Fomin, listed in the diplomatic blue book as one of several Soviet Embassy counselors. He invited Scali to meet him for lunch immediately. The two had lunched together on more serene occasions, though never before on such short notice. Scali explained that he was busy. Fomin pleaded: "It's very important. Meet me at the Occidental in ten minutes."

Scali went to the restaurant on Pennsylvania Avenue, guided perhaps by his long-term suspicion that Fomin was something more than a counselor of embassy. American security men considered him a big fish. They said he was a KGB colonel, the chief of Soviet intelligence operations in the United States.

Fomin seemed highly agitated. "The situation is very serious," he said. "Something must be done." As soon as the waiter had taken their orders, Fomin outlined a startling proposal.

Would the State Department be interested, he asked, in settling the missiles crisis on these terms:

1. The missile sites would be dismantled and shipped back to the Soviet Union under United Nations supervision.
2. Fidel Castro would pledge himself to accept no offensive weapons in the future.
3. The United States would pledge itself not to invade Cuba.

Scali replied that he could not speak for the United States Government. It was his personal feeling that such a proposal could be discussed. Fomin said if Adlai Stevenson were to pursue this line at the United Nations he would discover that Zorin was interested. He urged Scali to take the matter up at once with the State Department.

Racing back from the restaurant, Scali went to the office of Roger Hilsman, then State Department intelligence chief, and there dictated a memorandum of his conversation with Fomin. There was some debate among the experts in Hilsman's office as they tried to decide whether this extraordinary unofficial approach could be taken seriously. There had been other crisis communications between Moscow and Washington through a variety of channels: letters exchanged between Kennedy and Khrushchev; informal conversations between Ambassador Dobrynin and Robert Kennedy, between Khrushchev and the visiting American businessman, William Knox of Westinghouse International. Now a Soviet official, believed to be a senior intelligence agent masquerading as a diplomat, was confiding to a television reporter what could be the first intimation that Khrushchev was searching for a way out. Fomin's feeler might prove to be a dud, but Hilsman felt that it was worth exploring. He marched Scali down the hall to Dean Rusk's office. The Secretary of State promptly wrote out a message on a yellow, ruled pad, and, after clearing it with the White House, handed Scali a single sheet of paper in his own handwriting. "I want you to go back to this man and tell him this," Rusk said. The message was brief and pointed:

I have reason to believe that the USG [United States Government] sees real possibilities in this and supposes that representatives of the two governments could work this matter out with U Thant and with each other. My impression is, however, that time is very urgent.

At 7:35 P.M. Scali met Fomin in the coffee shop of the Statler Hilton Hotel, round the corner from the Soviet Embassy. He repeated Rusk's message, word for word.

Fomin asked the natural question: "Does this come from the highest sources?" Scali said Yes. "Are you absolutely certain?" Fomin asked again. Scali repeated his assurance. At this, Fomin said he must communicate immediately with the highest authorities in Moscow and rushed off.

By the time Scali had returned to the State Department and searched out Hilsman, there was fresh word from Moscow. At 6 P.M. the teletype linking the State Department with the American Embassy in Moscow started chattering. It was another letter from Khrushchev to Kennedy, a long, argumentative letter showing unmistakable signs of alarm and, some thought, a willingness to negotiate for the removal of Soviet missiles from Cuba. "We read it with a microscope," Tommy Thompson recalls. There were long sections that could have been deleted, with no loss of meaning. But scattered through the seemingly interminable text, like raisins in a cake, were a number of promising suggestions. The letter bore the stamp of Khrushchev's own style and, for the first time since the night of October 15, Dean Rusk thought he saw light at the end of a long, black tunnel.

The text of this letter has never been published, although Rusk showed it to the Senate Foreign Relations Committee after the event, and copies were distributed to several Allied governments. Even in paraphrase it reads like the nightmare outcry of a frightened man.

The moment had come [Khrushchev wrote] to rise above petty passions and to stop the drift toward war before it was too late. Elections might seem important in some countries, but they were transient things. If war should break out, neither he nor Kennedy would have the power to stop it. [A long autobiographical passage followed in which Khrushchev recited the horrors of war as he had seen it in his own country, twice devastated by the Germans in his lifetime.]

It was obvious that he and Kennedy could not agree on the significance of the missiles in Cuba. Kennedy was mistaken to think of them as offensive weapons. As a "military man," the President ought to understand that missiles, like old-fashioned cannon, could be offensive or defensive weapons. Everything depended on the use that was made of them. A cannon was defensive if it were set up to defend a national frontier or a fortified zone. Only if a number of cannon were massed together, with sufficient troops behind them, did they become offensive in that they could clear the way for infantry to attack.

There was, however, no need to quarrel over definitions. It was apparent he would never be able to persuade Kennedy that the missiles in Cuba were defensive weapons. As a "military man," the President ought to understand that missiles alone, even a vast number of missiles of varying ranges and explosive power, could not be a means of attack. Missiles were nothing but a means of extermination. To attack, you needed troops. Unless it was backed up by troops, no missile—not even a missile carrying a 100-megaton nuclear warhead—could be offensive. The Soviet ships bound for Cuba carried the most innocent cargoes. American military people wrongly imagined that the ships carried weapons. The weapons Cuba needed were already there. The Americans might search, but they would find none in the ships now on the way.

Khrushchev appealed for good sense, repeating his assurance that the ships now sailing to Cuba carried no weapons at all. The weapons required to defend the island were already there. He would not pretend that the Soviet Union had shipped no weapons to Cuba. Not at all. Soviet weapons were indeed shipped to Cuba, but they had long since arrived.

He could not be sure that Kennedy would understand or believe him. But he asked the President to believe in himself, to agree that passions ought to be controlled on both sides. Because if the United States Navy were to stop the ships, that would be piracy. The Soviet Union would be forced to defend them, as it had the right to do under international law. Where this would lead no man could say.

The Soviet leader called for normalization of relations. He told of receiving U Thant's plea that Soviet ships should carry no armaments of any kind to Cuba, while the United States undertook not to stop or board them for a few days and negotiations went forward. The Soviet side was prepared to enter into such negotiations. The Secretary General's reasonable proposals might offer a way out of the crisis.

Why had the Russians sent missiles into Cuba? Khrushchev said he would be quite frank.

It was because there had been a landing at the Bay of Pigs [18 months earlier]. Cuba had been attacked and many Cubans had lost their lives. He had mentioned this to Kennedy at their Vienna meeting in June of 1961. The President had then assured him that the Bay of Pigs landing was a mistake. Khrushchev accepted the explanation. The President had repeated it, making the point that not all Chiefs of State were prepared to acknowledge their mistakes. Khrushchev honored such frankness. The Soviet leaders were no less courageous. They too had acknowledged the mistakes of the past—Stalin's mistakes—acknowledged and sharply condemned them.

The President had every right to be concerned with the peace and welfare of the American people. The Chairman of the Soviet Council of Ministers was no less concerned for his people. Both ought to be jointly concerned with saving the peace. Because war in modern conditions would be a world war, a catastrophe for mankind. Khrushchev then proposed that the President of the United States give assurance that he would not attack Cuba, nor allow others to attack, while withdrawing the fleet from the approaches to Cuba. If that were to happen, the situation would be transformed overnight.

Khrushchev admitted he had no mandate to speak for Fidel Castro. But he had reason to believe that if the President were to give a no-invasion pledge, and recall the American fleet, then Castro would demobilize his forces. At that point the problems of "the weapons which you call offensive" would appear in a different light.

He called for a statesmanlike approach: the Russians would solemnly assure the world that their ships carried no weapons of any kind. The President would promise not to invade Cuba with United States forces and to withhold support from any other force that might be planning such an invasion. Then there would be no further need to keep Soviet military specialists in Cuba. The reason for their being in Cuba would vanish.

"If you have not lost your self-control, and sensibly conceive what this might lead to," the Khrushchev letter concluded, "then, Mr. President, we and you ought not now to pull on the ends of the rope in which you have tied the knot of war, because the more we pull, the tighter the knot will be tied. And a moment may come when the knot will be tied so tight that even he who tied it will not have the strength to untie it, and then it will be necessary to cut that knot; and what that would mean is not for me to explain to you, because you yourself understand perfectly of what terrible forces our countries dispose.

"Consequently, if there is no intention to tighten that knot and thereby doom the world to the catastrophe of thermonuclear war, then let us not only relax the forces pulling on the ends of the rope, let us take measures to untie that knot. We [the leaders of the Soviet Union] are ready for this."

The secret letter arrived in four sections, having been translated from the Russian and coded at the American Embassy in Moscow. Bill Brubeck, then executive secretary of the State Department, carried it section by section into Rusk's office. There, George Ball and Llewellyn Thompson sat with the Secretary of State, reading and rereading the key passages of Khrushchev's somewhat confused text as it rattled off the teleprinters. They kept looking for the catch.

Rusk now sent for Acheson, to get his personal advice. The former Secretary of State was not impressed. The Russians, he predicted, would never go through with such a deal. Acheson agreed with the general view that Khrushchev must have written the letter himself. It bore none of the hallmarks of official processing. The style was too personal. The non sequiturs were so obvious that the State Department men, sipping Scotch in Rusk's seventh-floor office at C and Twenty-second Streets in Washington, could readily picture Khrushchev's stubby figure, tramping up and down his enormous Kremlin office behind the Spassky Gate in Moscow, dictating to a secretary the possible terms of his own capitulation. Then dispatching them without time for discussion or editorial polishing.

His language was sufficiently imprecise to allow more than one interpretation. Acheson felt that Khrushchev, at the moment of writing his letter, must have been "either tight or scared." He was troubled by the sudden optimism of Rusk and Thompson. "I felt we were too eager to liquidate this thing," Acheson recalls. "So long as we had the thumbscrew on Khrushchev, we should have given it another turn every day. We were too eager to make an agreement with the Russians. They had no business there [in Cuba] in the first place."

The optimists—and cautious optimists they were—

thought they could discern the shape of an eventual settlement. Khrushchev seemed to have no stomach for a direct confrontation. They felt he must have faced the prospect of escalation, reckoned the cost and found it so horrendous that he was now seeking an escape hatch. One encouraging element was the absence of any demand that the United States trade off its Jupiter missiles in Turkey or Italy for the Soviet missiles in Cuba. Khrushchev, however, talked only of declarations by other people: President Kennedy would declare there was to be no invasion of Cuba, Castro would "declare demobilization and would appeal to the people to get down to peaceful labor." Khrushchev would make no declaration. If Kennedy and Castro did as he proposed, "then the necessity for the presence of our military specialists in Cuba would disappear." There was something missing—a specific commitment that the Soviet missiles would be dismantled and a method of verifying their removal.

It was at this point that Roger Hilsman suggested rereading the Khrushchev letter in the light of Fomin's approach to John Scali earlier the same day. Fomin had spoken of assigning United Nations inspectors to make certain the Soviet missiles were in fact removed. Khrushchev had failed to mention any form of inspection. Perhaps the two fitted together, Khrushchev's extraordinary *cri de coeur* and Fomin's three-point formula. Perhaps they were meant to be read together, amounting in fact to a single offer from the Kremlin.

Khrushchev, perhaps, was offering—through a channel he could later disown if need be—a concession he did not dare put in writing. It could be his way of spelling out to the President, without commitment, the eventual shape of a settlement tolerable to both sides.

The Executive Committee reconvened at 10 P.M. in extraordinary session to consider the secret letter.

The decision was made to treat it as a bona fide proposal, meriting a serious reply. Further study was ordered to make sure that the text contained no booby traps. Hilsman set his Soviet affairs experts, Helmut Sonnenfeldt and Joseph Neubert, to analyzing the letter alongside the Scali-Fomin memorandum. They worked through the night. "The rest of us went to bed," George Ball remembers, "with a vast sense of relief."

*Now it can go either way.*
—JOHN F. KENNEDY to members of the Executive Committee, October 27, 1962

CHEERED by Khrushchev's apparent willingness to work out a reasonable settlement and refreshed by a few hours' untroubled sleep, the members of the Executive Committee trooped back to the White House at ten o'clock that cool, sunny morning. Their task was to draft a reply accepting the Soviet leader's wholly unexpected proposal that both sides should step back from the brink and then negotiate what Khrushchev called a statesmanlike solution. The secret letter of the night before was being treated as a serious communication from one head of state to another—in spite of its strange argumentation about offensive and defensive weapons, its rambling reminiscences of Russia at war, and the odd juxtaposition of Kennedy's readiness to admit his own blunder at the Bay of Pigs with Khrushchev's readiness to blame the dead Stalin "for those mistakes which had been committed during the history of our State." Llewellyn Thompson agreed with the Kremlin-watchers in Hilsman's office that Khrushchev might be looking for a safe exit, without loss of face. They were impressed, in the first place, by his quick acceptance of U Thant's plea that both sides should try to avoid a confrontation at sea; even more by the broad hint that he might be prepared to remove all Soviet missiles from Cuba in exchange for Kennedy's pledge not to invade the island. Finally, there was the highly encouraging

fact that Khrushchev had asked for no *quid pro quo*
in Turkey. There remained, as the demonologists
looked at the Soviet proposition, one possible hooker.
Conceivably, Khrushchev might be playing for time
until his missiles were ready to fire. To guard against
such a maneuver, the analysis they had labored
through the night to complete recommended that the
President, in his reply, should insist that work on the
missile sites must be stopped before negotiations
went forward.

The Executive Committee meeting started, as always, with John McCone's intelligence briefing, a
daily ritual of overpowering solemnity, so efficacious
in driving out frivolous thoughts that some of the
younger members had come to call it "saying grace."
Work on the missile sites was still going ahead, Mc-
Cone reported, with no sign of slackening. The President and his closest advisers had just turned to the
main business of drafting his reply to the secret letter when Radio Moscow started broadcasting a second
Khrushchev letter addressed to Kennedy.

Suddenly all the rosy calculations of Friday night
evaporated. Khrushchev was raising his price. If Kennedy wanted the Russians to remove their missiles
from Cuba, he would have to remove the American
missile bases from Turkey.

You are worried over Cuba [Khrushchev wrote].
You say that it worries you because it lies at a distance of 90 miles across the sea from the shores of the
United States. However, Turkey lies next to us. Our
sentinels are pacing up and down and watching each
other. Do you believe that you have the right to demand security for your country, and the removal of
such weapons that you qualify as offensive, while not
recognizing this right for us?

You have stationed devastating rocket weapons,
which you call offensive, in Turkey, literally right
next to us. How then does recognition of our equal
military possibilities tally with such unequal relations

between our great states? This does not tally at all. . . .

This is why I make this proposal: we agree to remove those weapons from Cuba which you regard as
offensive weapons. We agree to do this and to state
this commitment in the United Nations. Your representatives will make a statement to the effect that
the United States, on its part, bearing in mind the
anxiety and concern of the Soviet state, will evacuate
its analogous weapons from Turkey. Let us reach an
understanding on what time you and we need to put
this into effect.

After this, representatives of the U.N. Security
Council could control on-the-spot the fulfillment of
these commitments. . . .

Khrushchev added, as if to reassure President Kennedy, that the missiles in Cuba were controlled by
Soviet officers, not Cubans. "Therefore," he said, "any
accidental use of them whatsoever to the detriment
of the United States of America is excluded."

Moscow Radio was still broadcasting Khrushchev's
bombshell when a second one landed. About 10:15
that morning, Major Rudolf Anderson, Jr., one of the
two U.S. Air Force pilots who had captured on film
the first hard proof of the Soviet missile build-up,
was brought down over Cuba in his U-2 plane. It
was clear that he had been shot out of the sky by
Soviet missilemen and, as Khrushchev had just finished telling the President, it was no accident. A dangerous new element had been added to the equation: the surface-to-air missiles installed by the Russians were now operational.

The second letter, just broadcast even though the
official text had not yet arrived from Moscow, was
markedly different in style and tone from the secret
letter of Friday. It seemed apparent to the worried
men around the big table in the Cabinet Room that
the Friday letter had been written by a different
hand, Khrushchev's own hand. The Saturday letter
bore the telltale signs of group thinking, Kremlin

style. Which of the two could be taken as genuine?
Which warranted a serious reply?

For a few minutes, the men around the President
gave free rein to their imaginations. They speculated
that Khrushchev might have been overruled or out-
voted in the Soviet Presidium. Maybe he was no
longer in control of Soviet policy. How else could
they explain this apparent repudiation of his own secret letter, sent less than twenty-four hours earlier?
Conceivably other members of the Presidium had discovered the secret letter, and had simply forced
Khrushchev to raise the ante by holding a pistol to
his head. Llewellyn Thompson, until that dismal
morning, had been reasonably confident that he was
reading the signs out of Moscow correctly. Although
his self-confidence was now shaken, Thompson could
not accept the lurid speculations about a revolt inside the Kremlin. He guessed that the Soviet leaders
had not been of one mind on how to wind up the
crisis; some among them might have felt that Khrushchev was letting Kennedy off too cheaply, that if the
Russians pushed just a bit harder the President
might agree to trade off the Jupiter missiles in Turkey for the Soviet missiles in Cuba. It was possible
that they had misread Walter Lippmann's column of
Thursday morning, leaping to the wrong conclusion
that the columnist was privy to the President's
thoughts. The Russians almost certainly knew that
Bruno Kreisky, the Austrian Foreign Minister, had
talked in the same vein before the Parliamentary frac-
tion of his own Socialist Party in Vienna. Moreover,
there had been a lot of gossip in the corridors of
the United Nations about a Cuba-Turkey exchange.

On the surface, the idea had a glittering symmetry.
Thompson warned that the Russians would certainly
interpret the President's acceptance as proof of weakness in Washington. Dean Rusk suggested that Turkey should reject the Soviet demand, although it had
been addressed to Kennedy. Let the Turks declare,

Rusk said, that they are members of the North Atlantic alliance, that the Jupiters are part of NATO's defenses, and that the current threat to peace is half a world away—in Cuba, not in Turkey. There was general agreement that no matter how little the Turkish missiles might be worth, in the military sense, to trade them off now would be to undermine the faith of the whole alliance in America's pledged word.

The President was trying hard all this time to suppress an inner rage. He distinctly remembered having given instructions, long before the Cuban missiles crisis, that the Jupiters must be removed from Turkey. Now he was confronted with one of two cruel choices: to shake, perhaps to shatter, the Western Alliance by trading off Turkey's missile defenses for the sake of United States security, or to risk thermonuclear war over some nearly obsolete missiles the United States had long since written off as militarily worthless.

The Russians could not have known that, soon after his Inauguration in January 1961, the President himself had raised the question at a National Security Council meeting. A big push was on at the Pentagon to replace first-generation missiles like Thor and Jupiter with Minuteman and Polaris by way of building what the military theoreticians called a "second-strike capacity." The Joint Congressional Committee on Atomic Energy had just recommended the removal of all Jupiters from Italy as well as Turkey. The Committee held that they were unreliable, inaccurate, obsolete and too easily sabotaged. What do we gain by leaving them there? the President had asked. Why be provocative?

The 1961 Berlin crisis had intervened. Kennedy and his policy planners found themselves preoccupied with other, seemingly more urgent problems. Then, in the late winter and early spring of 1962, an Administration study confirmed the Congressional Committee's findings. "Those Turkish missiles aren't

worth much," the President had said to Adlai Stevenson. "What the Turks want and need is the American
payrolls those bases represent." Dean Rusk was assigned to sound out the Turkish and Italian foreign
ministers during the NATO meeting at Oslo in May
1962. Paul Nitze went with him, representing the Defense Department. The Turkish Foreign Minister,
Selim Sarper, told Rusk and Nitze the Jupiters were
an indispensable token of America's commitment to
defend its allies. Too few Polaris submarines had
been commissioned at the time to permit stationing
them in the Mediterranean as replacements for the
Jupiters. So the matter was dropped, temporarily.

Late that summer the President inquired again
about the Turkish Jupiter bases. Rusk was in Europe.
In his absence, George Ball reported that the State
Department felt it would be unwise to press the matter further. The President disagreed. He then and
there directed that the missiles must be removed,
even at some political cost to the United States. Ball
and Nitze talked it over with the Turkish Ambassador in Washington and once more the reaction was
negative. The Ambassador warned that removal of the
missiles would have a most harmful effect on public
opinion in Turkey. Nothing happened. Though the
President, apparently, dismissed the Jupiters from
his mind, assuming that they were about to be removed, as ordered.

It was, therefore, with a doubled sense of shock
that Kennedy heard the news that Saturday morning.
Not only were the missiles still in Turkey but they
had just become pawns in a deadly chess game. Kennedy reflected sadly on the built-in futilities of big
government, and, in the struggle to control his emo-
tions, left the room. Ken O'Donnell knew the President sometimes vented his irritations through physi-
cal movement. He followed him out to the terrace
and they walked back and forth, talking together. A
few minutes afterward, O'Donnell telephoned Brom-

ley Smith, McGeorge Bundy's deputy in charge of National Security Council matters. "The President wants to know," O'Donnell said, "when he first asked for this thing." After quickly checking the file of National Security Council action memoranda, Smith was able to confirm the President's recollection. Kennedy had, indeed, issued instructions for removal of the Jupiters in the third week of August 1962, two months before the crisis.

The President recognized that it was too late now for lamentations over what might have been. He sensed at once that the Turkish missiles were a side issue. If, in the end, he had to order an armed attack on Cuba, leading perhaps to general war, it would not be because the United States five years before had stationed Jupiter missiles in Turkey. It would be because the Russians had tried by stealth to alter the balance of forces between East and West in the year 1962. The President believed Khrushchev must be forced to retreat and he felt justified in running considerable risks to achieve that retreat. It was one thing to discuss the liquidation of overseas bases around the conference table, in the framework of a general disarmament conference; quite another thing to sacrifice the Turkish bases under threat from Soviet missiles in Cuba trained on the United States.

Saturday was the longest, blackest day of the missiles crisis. The blockade, it must be remembered, had been the President's first option. If it failed to dislodge the missiles from Cuba more drastic steps would have to be taken in a matter of hours. The Executive Committee had not formally decided whether step number two would be an air strike against the Soviet missile sites, followed by an invasion of Cuba. But as the day wore on, this began to emerge as the most likely alternative.

"It was generally agreed," Pierre Salinger recalls, "that we couldn't go beyond Sunday without a further decision. At the very least, in my opinion, that would

have been a decision to take out the missile sites
by air attack. The thought was never far from the
President's mind that an air strike by itself would not
do the job. Earlier in the week he had put the question: 'If we had an air strike today, how soon would
we have to follow up with an invasion force?' The
answer the President got, as I recall it, was 'five to
six days.' What kept the urgency high was the continued work on the missile sites. We felt they could
be operational within a matter of hours. Then there
would be nothing left but to take them out and run
whatever risks that entailed."

McNamara adds: "The air strike was ready to go in
forty-eight hours; if pressed we could have done it
in thirty hours. Though air strike would not have been
my next recommendation. I had told Ros Gilpatric
[Deputy Secretary of Defense] that I would recommend deferring the air-strike option. I would have
added POL [petroleum products] to the contraband list and tightened the blockade instead. As the
SAM sites were already operational, I felt that would
be a less risky form of pressure. If it came to that,
I would rather have sunk a Russian ship than bombed
the missile sites."

Early that afternoon, Dean Rusk asked Roger Hilsman to carry over to the White House a proposed
State Department draft of the President's reply to
Khrushchev. He handed the document to McGeorge
Bundy, who read it quickly, then put it aside. Hilsman was on his way, passing through the West Executive Entrance of the White House, when a guard
grabbed his arm. There was an urgent call from his
office at the State Department. Hilsman blanched
when he heard that a second American U-2 plane,
on an air-sampling mission from Alaska to the North
Pole, had overflown the Chokut Peninsula. Soviet
fighters, based on Wrangel Island, had scrambled to
intercept the intruder. U.S. fighter planes from Alas-

ka were in the air at the moment trying to find the
U-2 plane and escort it back safely.

Hilsman raced back into the Executive Mansion.
He found the President with Bundy in Mrs. Lincoln's
office and gave them an agitated account of the latest intelligence. In the current emergency, with Soviet armed forces in a state of mobilization, it was
easy to see the perilous implications of that stray
flight over Soviet territory. The President, who had
issued careful instructions against provocative flights
of this sort, was moved to ironic laughter.* Reminded
perhaps of his wasted foresight in ordering the Jupiters removed from Turkey, he said: "There is always
some so-and-so who doesn't get the word."

All through the morning and into the afternoon the
Executive Committee wrestled with the problem of
answering Khrushchev in such a way as to get the
confrontation back on the political track. Adlai Stevenson had been the first of the President's advisors
to warn of the possibility that the Russians would
try to bring the Turkish missile bases into the bargaining. The President himself had tried to get them
out of Turkey months before the crisis. The free-
wheeling discussion that Saturday canvassed every
possible approach short of submitting to Khrushchev's demand. Although Stevenson has since been
identified as the chief advocate, men with established
reputations for cold-war toughness turned their
minds that afternoon to ingenious devices for removing the Turkish missiles from the equation without
seeming to accept Khrushchev's terms. There was talk
round the table of a maneuver by which the Turkish Government would somehow be persuaded to
petition the United States for their removal. Finally,

* The following day Khrushchev wrote to Kennedy: "What is
this, a provocation? One of your planes violates our frontier
during this anxious time we are both experiencing, when everything has been put into combat readiness. Is it not a fact that
an intruding American plane could be easily taken for a
nuclear bomber, which might push us to a fateful step?"

the discussion settled on a new concept. The Executive Committee agreed that the United States could afford to pay a considerable price in subsequent negotiations if the Russians would stop their Cuba missile build-up at once, before the IRBM's became operational. The concession was to be disguised as part of a broader negotiation with the Russians concerning relaxation of tensions beween NATO and the Warsaw Pact. Accordingly, the President talked privately with Rusk and McNamara at the close of the morning session and then assigned Gilpatric to spend the afternoon in Bundy's basement office at the White House, with representatives of the State Department and the Joint Chiefs of Staff, writing a "scenario" for the early removal of all Jupiter missiles from Turkey and Italy. There were to be two separate plans in view of the differing national circumstances as between Turks and Italians. Gilpatric's scenario was to be ready for the Executive Committee's third metting of the day at 9 P.M.

It was in the light of this unreported decision accepting the removal of the Jupiter bases as a legitimate goal of subsequent negotiations that the White House, on Saturday afternoon, issued a public statement not so much rejecting as postponing Khrushchev's demand:

Several inconsistent and conflicting proposals have been made by the U.S.S.R. within the last 24 hours, including the one just made public in Moscow. The proposal broadcast this morning involves the security of nations outside the Western Hemisphere. But it is the Western Hemisphere countries and they alone that are subject to the threat that has produced the current crisis—the action of the Soviet Government in secretly introducing offensive weapons into Cuba. Work on those offensive weapons is still proceeding at a rapid pace. The first imperative must be to deal with this immediate threat, under which no sensible negotiations can proceed.

It is, therefore, the position of the United States that as an urgent preliminary to consideration of any proposals, work on the Cuban bases must stop; offensive weapons must be rendered inoperable; and further shipments of offensive weapons to Cuba must cease—all under effective international control.

As to proposals concerning the security of nations outside this hemisphere, the United States and its allies have long taken the lead in seeking properly inspected arms limitations, on both sides. These efforts can continue as soon as the present Soviet-created threat is ended.

At 3:35 P.M. the Defense Department belatedly announced that a reconnaissance plane (Major Anderson's U-2) was missing over Cuba, its pilot presumed lost.

At 4 P.M. the Joint Chiefs of Staff advised the Commander in Chief, Atlantic, that the Caribbean interception area would be defined by a pair of intersecting circles of 500-mile radius, one centered on Havana, the other on Cape Maysi. The message also was sent to the United Nations, so U Thant could inform the Soviet delegation. Zorin refused to accept it.

The Executive Committee had been meeting since 2:30 that afternoon in George Ball's conference room at the State Department. At 4 P.M. its members went to the White House so the President could weigh the sobering evidence collected so far. There had been the loss of Major Anderson and his U-2. Two more reconnaissance planes had drawn antiaircraft fire as they swooped low over the missile sites that morning. In addition there had been the accidental overflight of Soviet territory in the far north. The President promptly accepted Dean Rusk's suggestion that nothing should be said in public about the stray flight over the Chokut Peninsula unless the Russians publicized it first. He also decided that Cuban surveillance flights would have to be continued, with fighter escorts if the shooting continued. There remained the delicate matter of replying to Khrushchev's secret letter.

It was Robert Kennedy who had suggested first brushing aside the broadcast letter and then responding to the secret letter of Friday night as if it were a valid proposal. Rusk, Ball, Thompson and Bundy —all had put their hands to various drafts. The Attorney General complained that each of the early drafts seemed to miss the opportunity of the moment. Then the President asked his younger brother to try. "If you disagree so violently, go draft one yourself," the President said. Robert Kennedy agreed, took Ted Sorensen and the rejected drafts with him into an adjoining room, and, a few minutes before seven o'clock that evening, handed the President a new version. This was the draft President Kennedy dispatched to Khrushchev at 8:05 P.M. Saturday. Salinger handed copies to the White House reporters at the same time. The essence of the final approach to Moscow was to gamble that Khrushchev had not been overruled since sending off the secret letter. The President, in effect, accepted a set of terms Khrushchev had never formally offered. Robert Kennedy and Sorensen had plucked from the secret letter, the Scali-Fomin memorandum, and the broadcast letter of Saturday, those elements that were acceptable to the United States. And the President was accepting them in full view of the anxious world.

Dear Mr. Chairman [Kennedy wrote]:
I have read your letter of October 26th with great care and welcomed the statement of your desire to seek a prompt solution to the problem. The first thing that needs to be done, however, is for work to cease on offensive missile bases in Cuba and for all weapons systems in Cuba capable of offensive use to be rendered inoperable, under effective United Nations arrangements.

Assuming this is done promptly, I have given my representatives in New York instructions that will permit them to work out this week end—in co-operation with the Acting Secretary General and your representative—an arrangement for a permanent solution to the Cuban problem along the lines suggested in your letter of October 26th. As I read your letter, the key elements of your proposals—which seem generally acceptable as I understand them—are as follows:

1. You would agree to remove these weapons systems from Cuba under appropriate United Nations observation and supervision; and undertake, with suitable safeguards, to halt the further introduction of such weapons systems into Cuba.

2. We, on our part, would agree—upon the establishment of adequate arrangements through the United Nations to ensure the carrying out and continuation of these commitments—(*a*) to remove promptly the quarantine measures now in effect, and (*b*) to give assurances against an invasion of Cuba. I am confident that other nations of the Western Hemisphere would be prepared to do likewise.

If you will give your representative similar instructions, there is no reason why we should not be able to complete these arrangements and announce them to the world within a couple of days. The effect of such a settlement on easing world tensions would enable us to work toward a more general arrangement regarding "other armaments," as proposed in your second letter, which you made public. I would like to say again that the United States is very much interested in reducing tensions and halting the arms race; and if your letter signifies that you are prepared to discuss a detente affecting NATO and the Warsaw Pact, we are quite prepared to consider with our allies any useful proposals.

But the first ingredient, let me emphasize, is the cessation of work on missile sites in Cuba and measures to render such weapons inoperable, under effective international guarantees. The continuation of this threat, or a prolonging of this discussion concerning Cuba by linking these problems to the broader questions of European and world security, would surely lead to an intensification of the Cuban crisis and a grave risk to the peace of the world. For this reason, I hope we can quickly agree along the lines outlined in this letter and in your letter of October 26th.

JOHN F. KENNEDY

To be absolutely certain that Khrushchev fully understood the grave warning embedded in the final paragraph, Robert Kennedy delivered a copy of the President's letter to Ambassador Dobrynin at the Soviet Embassy on 16th Street. Kennedy emphasized to the Ambassador that time was running out. He said the United States was ready to begin military action by the first of the week. (In fact the Air Force was prepared to bomb the missile sites in Cuba Tuesday morning.) Visibly shaken, Dobrynin gave it as his personal opinion that the Soviet leaders were so deeply committed they would have to reject the President's terms. Kennedy once more stressed the urgency of an immediate affirmative response. Other U-2s would be flying over Cuba the next day, he said, and it would be dangerous if the Russians fired upon them. Dobrynin made no effort to disguise his own pessimism. The Kremlin, he repeated, was deeply committed.

At 9 P.M. the Executive Committee held its third meeting of the day. There was still no explanation for the apparent change of signals in Moscow, and, in Cuba, the Soviet antiaircraft missiles had drawn first blood. The President and the men sitting with him at the long Cabinet table that night were no more optimistic than the Soviet Ambassador. They had just served an ultimatum, giving Khrushchev a few hours to retreat with some semblance of dignity. If he refused it could be war. There was talk of the next step: tightening the blockade to keep Soviet petroleum out of Cuba or launching an air attack to destroy the Soviet missiles on the ground. No decisions were made, escept to call up twenty-four troop carrier squadrons of the Air Force Reserve. McNamara announced the call to active duty at 9:20 P.M. The troop carriers would be needed if—as the President had feared all along—it became necessary to invade Cuba. The latest contingency plan estimated that 60,000 to 100,000 ground force troops would be needed. The Army and Marine Corps units were already in Florida or in the Panama Canal Zone. This was no bluff.

Before adjourning the meeting, Kennedy arranged with McNamara to review the air-strike planning at nine o'clock on Sunday morning—an hour before the Executive Committee reconvened. General Sweeney was to be there, along with McNamara and Maxwell Taylor. As the meeting broke up close to midnight, the President said, wearily: "Now it can go either way."

*Success has a hundred fathers and defeat is
an orphan.*
—JOHN F. KENNEDY, recalling the Bay of
Pigs disaster

SUNDAY DAWNED in surpassing glory, the golden October sunshine strangely out of keeping with the macabre expectations of the men around the President. The morning was so beautiful that George Ball said to McNamara as they walked into the White House: "It reminds me of the Georgia O'Keefe painting that has a rose growing out of an ox skull." The Secretary of Defense knew precisely what the Under Secretary of State was talking about. Passing the Jefferson Memorial on his way back to the Pentagon Saturday evening, McNamara had remarked the spectacular beauty of the setting sun over the Potomac. He remembers wondering how many more sunsets he was destined to see. Even Tommy Thompson, outwardly the most self-controlled of professional diplomats, had broken a lifetime rule that evening by giving way to his anxieties. If he should not come home the following day—the Ambassador-at-Large had said to his wife, Jane—he would at the first opportunity let her know where she and the Thompson daughters were to join him when the capital was evacuated.

President Kennedy's last letter to Nikita Khrushchev had, after all, been a shot in the dark. The President had eagerly accepted a proposition the Russian had never formally offered. And the Soviet Ambassador had warned Robert Kennedy that, in his opinion, the Kremlin was far too deeply committed to accept. Early Sunday morning, prepared for the worst, the Defense Department announced the call to duty of additional Air Force reserve squadrons. The Cuban overflights were going ahead and there still was no sign of slackening in the work of making the Russian missiles ready to fire. A few minutes before nine o'clock Washington time, Moscow Radio announced that it would broadcast an important statement on the hour. The men around the President waited for Khrushchev's reply, speculating morosely that, if No was the answer, the United States would have to launch an air strike no later than Tuesday morning. Then the announcer in Moscow started reading another Khrushchev letter, the tenth letter that had passed between the White House and the Kremlin in seven days—five each way. The wire-service reporters in Moscow did not have long to wait for their lead. It was in the third paragraph:

In order to eliminate as rapidly as possible the conflict which endangers the cause of peace, to give an assurance to all people who crave peace, and to reassure the American people who, I am certain, also want peace, as do the people of the Soviet Union, *the Soviet Government,* in addition to earlier instructions on the discontinuation of further work on weapons construction sites, *has given a new order to dismantle the arms which you described as offensive, and to crate and return them to the Soviet Union.*

There followed six paragraphs of tortured self-justification having to do with Castro's fears that his country was about to be invaded, and the unexceptionable motives of his Russian protectors in having sent missiles to Cuba "to prevent rash acts," such as the recent shelling by a Cuban exiles' ship. Khrushchev then repeated and accepted the terms Kennedy had set Saturday night:

I regard with respect and trust the statement you made in your message of 27 October, 1962, that there would be no attack, no invasion of Cuba, and not only on the part of the United States, but also of other nations of the Western Hemisphere, as you said in your message. Then the motives which induced us to render assistance of such a kind to Cuba disappear.

It is for this reason that we instructed our officers— these means, as I had already informed you earlier, are in the hands of Soviet officers—to take appropriate measures to discontinue construction of the aforementioned facilities, to dismantle them, and to return them to the Soviet Union. As I had informed you in the letter of 27 October, we are prepared to reach agreement to enable the U.N. representatives to verify the dismantling of these means. Thus, in view of the assurances you have given and our instructions on dismantling, there is every condition for eliminating the present conflict.

Khrushchev added that in place of Ambassador Zorin (who at the height of the crisis had made an enemy of U Thant by accusing him of pro-Western sympathies) he was sending V. V. Kuznetsov, First Deputy Foreign Minister of the Soviet Union, to work with Thant in "his noble efforts aimed at eliminating the present dangerous crisis."

Robert Kennedy got the word directly from Dobrynin—a new, smiling Dobrynin this time—who strode into the Attorney General's office that Sunday morning bearing new assurances. Everything was going to be all right, he said. The President would be satisfied with Khrushchev's fulfillment of the promises made in his latest letter. The missiles would indeed be dismantled, crated, and shipped home to Russia. Chairman Khrushchev, moreover, sent best wishes to the President and to his brother, the Attorney General.

The official text of Khrushchev's letter had been delivered to the American Embassy at 7 P.M. Moscow time (10 A.M. in Washington). It would take hours to reach the State Department. The President decided not to wait for the official text. At noon, after an hour-long session with the Executive Committee in a mood of unaccustomed exhilaration, he drafted a quick acceptance statement. It was released to the White House reporters and beamed to Moscow over the Voice of America:

I welcome Chairman Khrushchev's statesmanlike decision to stop building bases in Cuba, dismantling offensive weapons and returning them to the Soviet Union under United Nations verification. This is an important and constructive contribution to peace.

We shall be in touch with the Secretary General of the United Nations with respect to reciprocal measures to assure peace in the Caribbean area.

It is my earnest hope that the governments of the world can, with the solution of the Cuban crisis, turn their urgent attention to the compelling necessity for ending the arms race and reducing world tensions. This applies to the military confrontation between the Warsaw Pact and NATO countries as well as to other situations in other parts of the world where tensions lead to the wasteful diversion of resources to weapons of war.

Kennedy held his formal reply until the official text had been delivered. He could not conceal from the men in the Cabinet Room, who had sat with him through other crisis decisions, the sudden change in himself. "He was a different guy that morning," Don Wilson recalls. "He walked with a lighter step."

Inevitably, Kennedy's relief at having turned the most dangerous corner of his Presidency was tempered by his awareness of Soviet commitments yet to be redeemed, and his appreciation of how difficult it must have been for Khrushchev to back down. He therefore cautioned his advisers against premature jubilation. At 1:04 P.M., Dean Rusk carried the President's cautionary words to the State Department press corps. Speaking off the record, by way of guidance for the reporters, Rusk said: "If there is a debate, a rivalry, a contest going on in the Kremlin over how to play this situation, we don't want the word 'capitulation' used or any gloating in Washington to strengthen the hands of those in Moscow who wanted to play this another way." As for the continuing headache that Cuba had represented long before Soviet missiles were introduced, Rusk was frank. "I think we will still have a Cuban problem on our hands," he said, although he saw a possibility that following the removal of the missiles Fidel Castro might not appear so great a menace to the hemisphere. There remained, however, the sticky problem of getting U.N. inspectors into Cuba to certify the removal of the Russian missiles; and the President's insistence that the removal of offensive weapons meant removing the Ilyushin bombers as well as the medium- and inter-mediate-range missiles. "It is not yet the time to say this is over," Rusk concluded.

Castro had just issued a declaration of independence, completely ignoring the Soviet decision to withdraw the missiles under U.N. inspection. He broadcast his own set of terms for winding up the crisis. Castro demanded of the United States that it should: (1) end the blockade and all economic pressures on Cuba; (2) end all harassments of his regime by Cuban exiles; (3) stop the raids by exile commando groups; (4) stop the overflights of Cuban territory; and (5) withdraw from Guantánamo Bay. It was clear that Khrushchev had not consulted Castro before backing down and that Fidel felt betrayed by his "socialist ally."

Nevertheless, at 1:30 on Sunday afternoon, the Joint Chiefs of Staff sent a new directive to Admiral Dennison's Atlantic command. There was to be no boarding of ships or any other forceful action. The quarantine ships would remain on station, awaiting further orders.

At that hour, four Administration officials were on their way to New York, hoping that U Thant could be persuaded to order an immediate start on the inspection the Russians had just promised. The Administration had quickly examined the technical requirements, deciding the job could be done by air, from C-130 transport planes, flying low over the missile sites with their doors open. The planes were standing by at Air Force bases in Georgia. Orders went out to have their silvery skins painted white, with U.N. markings. Canada had agreed to supply experienced pilots. The four officials—Michael Forrestal of the White House staff, Joseph Charyk, Under Secretary of the Air Force; Abram Chayes and Joseph Siscoe of the State Department—reached U.N. headquarters about 2:30 that afternoon. Pickets were still parading in the United Nations Plaza with placards denouncing the blockade. Apparently the word of Khrushchev's retreat had not reached them. The four Washington officials talked at length with Stevenson, who told them he did not believe Thant could be persuaded to act on his own authority. Stevenson made it clear that he had no intention of talking tough to Thant. And the Secretary General, as predicted, refused. To move now, he said, would be to exceed his powers.

Washington took no very tragic view of this failure to push on the hands of the clock. The immediate crisis was past, the imminent danger of war averted. There would certainly be disappointments ahead in the long, hard negotiations now agreed upon. None of these could detract from the President's victory for peace which—by his own strict injunction—was not to be called a victory.

That afternoon the President drafted and dispatched to Moscow a more formal reply to Khrushchev's Sunday morning letter.

I think that you and I, with our heavy responsibilities for the maintenance of peace [Kennedy wrote], were aware that developments were reaching a point where events could have become unmanageable. . . .

I consider my letter to you of October 27 and your reply of today as firm undertakings on the part of both our governments which should be promptly carried out. . . .

Mr. Chairman, both of our countries have great unfinished tasks and I know that your people as well as those of the United States can ask for nothing better than to pursue them free from the fear of war. . . .

I agree with you that we must devote urgent attention to the problem of disarmament, as it relates to the whole world and also to critical areas. Perhaps now, as we step back from danger, we can together make real progress in this vital field. I think we should give priority to questions relating to the proliferation of nuclear weapons, on earth and in outer space, and to the great effort for a nuclear test ban.*

That night the Kennedy brothers sat together talking of the crisis. The President mentioned Barbara Tuchman's book, *The Guns of August,* and the miscalculations that had led the Great Powers to stumble into the 1914 war. "Tell me how it happened," he recited. "Oh, if we ever knew." Some day, the President supposed, someone would write a book about "the Missiles of October." Together, the Kennedys reviewed incidents of the thirteen October days that had lodged in their memory. There was the time that U-2 brought back photographs of Cuban Air Force planes lined up on an airfield like soldiers on parade. Maxwell Taylor had scoffed at this Cuban foolishness. A few well-placed bombs would wipe them out. The President sternly reminded Taylor that if anyone had taken the trouble to photograph certain United States air bases he might perhaps have found the planes lined up with equal symmetry.

At last, John Kennedy said: "Maybe this is the night I should go to the theater." Both brothers laughed uproariously. Both were thinking of Ford's Theater.

* On August 5, 1963, in an elaborate Kremlin ceremony, a new treaty banning all nuclear tests except those held underground was signed by Rusk, Gromyko and Lord Home.

TWENTY-THREE DAYS PASSED. The same Russians who had built the missile bases now smashed the concrete footings with electric hammers, plowed up the ground and loaded their missiles on ships bound for the Black Sea and Baltic ports whence they had come. But Castro refused to give up the Ilyushin bombers which, unlike the missiles, were under his control. The ships of Admiral Ward's task force remained on station in the Caribbean. General Power kept his loaded B-52s in the air. Key West was still bulging with troops. The President, advised by Tommy Thompson that Khrushchev would yield in the end, stepped up the pressure. At the United Nations, and also in private meetings of Robert Kennedy with Dobrynin, the Russians were told time and again that unless they removed the bombers the President would feel free to take military action; the no-invasion deal was off so long as a single offensive weapon remained on Cuban soil.

On November 20—Robert Kennedy's thirty-seventh birthday—Dobrynin called on the Attorney General. "I have a birthday present for you," he said. It was another letter from Khrushchev to the President, agreeing to remove the bombers. Robert Kennedy asked the Soviet Ambassador to point out the significant passages in Khrushchev's text. Dobrynin marked them carefully. Then he marched up and down the Attorney General's office, re-enacting the scene in Khrushchev's office as he had observed the First Secretary and Chairman of the Soviet Council of Ministers dictating other important messages in the past. A new bargain was struck: the President, Robert Ken-

nedy assured Dobrynin, would issue his no-invasion
pledge within thirty days if the bombers started moving out. The President, that same day, announced
Khrushchev's promise to remove the bombers, adding
that all known launching sites in Cuba had now been
dismantled and the missiles sent back to the Soviet
Union. In the circumstances, the President gave orders to terminate the quarantine. All told, nineteen
Soviet merchant ships and six belonging to other
Communist-bloc countries had passed through the
screen of American destroyers; apart from twenty-
three ships registered in other countries that were
sailing under Soviet-bloc charters and seven belonging to friendly nations—three Greek, two British, one
Spanish, and one Italian. The quarantine had been in
force exactly twenty-seven days.

It was Fidel Castro, not Khrushchev, who had
balked at the settlement terms. "Whoever comes to
inspect Cuba," he shouted, "must come in battle ar-
ray." U Thant had tried halfheartedly to bring him
around, flying to Havana on October 30. He had returned the following day with nothing to show but
his notes of an interminable Castro harangue directed
against the Russians no less than the Americans.
Thant's approach to Castro was apologetic. The Acting Secretary General had talked at times as if he
represented forty-five nonaligned countries instead of
all the United Nations—Russia and the United States
included. "We hold this matter of inspection to be
one more attempt to humiliate our country, and for
that reason we do not accept it," Castro said. "I understand perfectly the sentiments of Your Excellency," Thant murmured. Throughout the conversation
Thant behaved as if he were carrying out a distasteful
duty forced upon him by the United States. If he
saw fit to mention that the Soviet Union also was
party to the U.N. inspection plan, an essential element in the Kennedy-Khrushchev agreement to wind
up the crisis, excerpts of the conversation published

afterward by the Cuban Government ignored that point. Castro had complained bitterly that the Russians treated him like a vassal, not allowing any Cuban to set foot on the missile bases, and—when the pressure became too much for them—agreeing to remove the missiles without asking his leave. No foreign government had the right, he argued, to speak in Cuba's name. There could be no inspection without Cuban consent and he refused to give it.

Khrushchev found himself in a tight box of his own construction: Castro was sulking, Kennedy threatening, and the Red Chinese were crowing over his "capitulation" to the imperialists. In Havana, posters proclaiming Cuba's eternal friendship for the Soviet Union were ripped from the walls. Street urchins sang a mocking couplet:

> *Nikita, Nikita,*   (Nikita, Nikita,
> *Lo que se da*     That which is given
> *No se quita.*     Is not taken back.)

Peking encouraged Castro to go on thumbing his nose at Moscow. The Chinese coined a Mao-Marxian syllogism to doubly denounce Khrushchev. It was sheer "adventurism," Peking said, to have put missiles into Cuba in the first place—a judgment millions in other countries could accept; but to take them out under American pressure amounted to simple "capitulationism."

As in other awkward moments—the moment in 1956, for example, when Budapest rebelled against Russian overlordship—Khrushchev sent for Anastas Mikoyan. On November 2, after a brief stopover in New York, the wily Mikoyan flew to Havana. His unquestioned talents as Moscow's great persuader were of no effect in Cuba. He pleaded, argued, threatened, but Castro would not be moved. For days on end, Castro simply ignored his distinguished visitor. "Mikoyan discovered that Castro was the first satellite he

couldn't dominate," said one American who kept in
close touch with the U.N. negotiations. "When he returned to New York he told us all about the beautiful
beaches and the wonderful agricultural stations he
had seen in the new Cuba. But it was quite obvious
that he failed with Castro." While Mikoyan was in
Havana, his wife died in Moscow. He missed the
funeral, staying on to wrestle with Fidel as the Kremlin had directed. In the end the missiles were inspected at sea on their way out of Cuba. Russian
captains cheerfully pulled back the tarpaulins while
United States destroyers alongside them kept their
running tally. They counted forty-two missiles altogether being removed to Russia. Navy reconnaissance
planes followed the ships back across the Atlantic to
make sure they did not change direction.

The sticking point for Khrushchev was the Ilyushin
bombers. These had been a gift. They were now Cuban property and Castro would not hear of sur-
rendering them. While Mikoyan grappled with Castro
in Havana, John McCloy met repeatedly with Kuznetsov—in New York, at his own home in Stamford,
Connecticut, or at the Soviet delegation's Glen Cove,
Long Island, estate. Both McCloy and Stevenson soon
wearied of the long, fruitless conversations with Kuznetsov. The Ilyushins in any case were obsolescent
planes and the Russians, some suggested, may have
been justified in arguing that they were not part of
the original bargain. Some sentiment developed in
the U.S. negotiating team to let Khrushchev wriggle
off the hook. But the President, giving personal attention to the detailed reports of each negotiating
session, refused. Instead, whenever a new snag developed, he would fire off one more letter to Khrushchev and step up the pressure, sending word through
one emissary or another that if the bombers were
not promptly removed the United States Air Force
would have to destroy them on the ground. Tommy
Thompson's reading had been that once Khrush-

chev backed down on the missiles, at whatever cost
to his own prestige, he would not forever go on balk-
ing at the removal of some over-age bombers as well.
The President acted on Thompson's advice to the end.
As for the Russians, they had been given reason to
believe that if a fire-fight started the Washington
"hawks" might overpower the "doves," invade Cuba
and get rid of Castro. They did not care for the
prospect. "We were happy to leave them believing
that could happen," one of the American negotiators
recalled. Again, Thompson's reading of the Kremlin
auguries proved triumphantly accurate. On November 19 Castro caved in, agreeing not to obstruct the
removal of the bombers. The following day Dobrynin
delivered his "birthday present" to Robert Kennedy.
Mikoyan left Cuba on November 25 with something
accomplished, after all. And, on December 6, the last
of the Ilyushins, neatly crated on the deck of a
Soviet ship, sailed home.

To each of the Executive Committee members Kennedy in gratitude presented a silver plaque in the
form of a calendar for the month of October 1962, the
thirteen crisis days etched more deeply than the rest.
There was no inscription, only the initials J.F.K. at the
upper right and the recipient's initials at the left. No
inscription was needed.

On December 12, 1962, speaking before the Su-
preme Soviet, Nikita Khrushchev attempted to set
down certain lessons of the Cuban missile crisis. He
put the question:

"Which side triumphed, who won? In this respect
one may say that it was sanity, the cause of peace and
security of peoples, that won. Both sides displayed a
sober approach and took into account that unless such
steps are taken as could help to overcome the dangerous development of events, a World War III might
break out.

"As a result of mutual concessions and compromise,
an understanding was reached which made it possible

to remove dangerous tension, to normalize the situation.

"It is, of course, true that the nature of imperialism has not changed. But imperialism today is no longer what it used to be when it held undivided sway over the world. If it is now a 'paper tiger,' those who say this know that this 'paper tiger' has atomic teeth. It can use them and it must not be treated lightly. . . .

"Of course, this was a critical time and the Government of the United States understood the possible development of events. . . .

"Both sides made concessions. We withdrew ballistic rockets and agreed to withdraw IL-28 planes. This gives satisfaction to the Americans. But both Cuba and the Soviet Union received satisfaction too: the American invasion of Cuba has been averted, the naval blockade lifted, the situation in the Caribbean is returning to normalcy."

President Kennedy preferred not to philosophize about the missile crisis, though he was frequently asked after the event to state his own conclusions. In a joint interview with the three television networks on December 17, the President talked of one lesson.

I think, looking back on Cuba [Kennedy said]; what is of concern is the fact that both governments were so far out of contact, really. I don't think that we expected that he [Khrushchev] would put the missiles in Cuba, because it would have seemed such an imprudent action for him to take, as it was later proved. Now, he obviously must have thought that he could do it in secret and that the United States would accept it. So that he did not judge our intentions accurately.

Well now, if you look at the history of this century, where World War I really came through a series of misjudgments of the intentions of others, certainly World War II where Hitler thought . . . that the British might not fight. . . .

When you look at all those misjudgments which brought on war, and then you see the Soviet Union

and the United States, so far separated in their be-
liefs . . . and you put the nuclear equation into that
struggle; that is what makes this . . . such a dangerous time. . . . One mistake can make this whole thing
blow up.

The President's crucial achievement, once the crisis
had started, was to make Khrushchev understand that
he must withdraw—by showing him the nuclear abyss
to the edge of which he had blundered and pointing a
way back without disgrace. In the nuclear age, every
President has the power to make war, with or without
a Congressional declaration. Every President has the
power to surrender a vital interest, with or without
Senate ratification. To this extent, megaton technology
has annihilated the clock and amended the Constitu-
tion. Kennedy succeeded in steering a safe course between war and surrender, remembering always that
Khrushchev too was a politician, who must never be
put in the position of risking discredit at home. Kennedy put the lesson this way in his American University speech the following summer:

Above all, while defending our own vital interests,
nuclear powers must avert those confrontations which
bring an adversary to the choice of either a humiliating retreat or a nuclear war.

It is, perhaps, a fitting epitaph.

Acheson, Dean, 33, 34, 45, 51–52, 54–55, 59, 73–74, 82, 87, 93–94, 96–97, 111, 162

Adenauer, Chancellor Konrad, 97, 111

Allen, Robert S., 70

Alpha 66, 68

Alsop, Joseph, 41

Alsop, Stewart, 57

Anderson, Adm. George W., 90, 123–124, 136–137

Anderson, Major Rudolf, 16, 167, 175

Arms Control and Disarmament Agency, 33, 70

Attwood, William, 119–120

*Aviation Week and Space Technology*, 4

Bahía de Cochinos, *see* Bay of Pigs

Ball, George, 22, 32, 51, 70, 83, 103, 109, 164, 170, 180

Bartlett, Charles, 57

Bay of Pigs, 5, 10, 23–25, 28, 34, 59, 160

Board of National Estimates, 12–13

Bohlen, Charles E., 19, 32, 41, 43, 127

Brubeck, William, 162

Bruce, David E. K., 87, 93–95, 111–112, 127

*Bucharest*, 140–141

Bundy, McGeorge, 3–4, 16, 19–20, 26, 31–32, 40, 64n, 67

*Canberra*, 124

Capehart, Sen. Homer E., 2

Carroll, Lt. Gen. Joseph, 15, 17, 18, 31

Carter, Gen. Marshall S., 12, 13, 16, 18, 32

Castro, Premier Fidel, 2, 6, 9, 184, 188–191

Castro, Raul, 6

Charyk, Joseph, 185

Chayes, Abram J., 59, 68, 98, 117, 185

Clark, William, 130

Cleveland, Harlan, 114

Cline, Ray, 13, 19

Committee on Overhead Reconnaissance (COMOR), 14–15

de Gaulle, President Charles, 96–97

Dennison, Adm. Robert L., 124, 155

Diefenbaker, Prime Minister John, 97

Dillon, Douglas, 7, 20, 32, 35, 66–67, 88, 91, 100

Dobrynin, Anatoliy, 8, 37, 103, 117, 121, 178, 182, 187–188

Dowling, Walter, 83

Dryfoos, Orvil, 92

Dubovik, Lt. Gen. Vladimir A., 116

Dulles, Allen, 28

Dulles, John Foster, 24

Eisenhower, Dwight D., 64, 133

ELITE (code name), 46

Ellender, Sen. Allen J., 119

Executive Committee, 33, 44, 65, 72, 78, 89, 98–99, 129, 142, 153, 163, 165, 173, 175, 178–179

Finletter, Thomas K., 93

Fleming, Robert, 98

Fomin, Alexander S., 156–158
Foreman, Ben, 117
Forrestal, Michael, 185
Foster, William C., 70
Frost, Robert, 24
Fulbright, Sen. J. William, 102

Gaitskell, Hugh, 120
Gilpatric, Roswell, 17, 26, 27n, 32, 38, 67, 135
Graham, Philip, 92
Gromyko, Andrei, 48, 60–65, 101
Guanajay, Cuba, 46, 75, 134
Guantánamo, Cuba, 11, 79
Guevara, Ernesto (Che), 8
*Guns of August, The,* 186

Halleck, Congressman Charles, 103
Harriman, Averell, 85
Hawk (antiaircraft missile), 70
Heyser, Richard S., 16
Hickory Hill University, 18
Hillenbrand, Martin, 85
Hilsman, Roger, 6, 21–22, 29, 32, 157, 163, 172
Holmes, Judge Oliver Wendell, 82
Hughes, Gov. Richard J., 141
Hughes, Thomas L., 141, 142

IL-28 (plane), 75, 134, 187, 192
Inchaustegui, Mario Garcia, 115
Ivanov, Capt. Eugene, 127–128, 146

*John R. Pierce,* 152
Johnson, Vice President Lyndon B., 32, 40, 50
Johnson, U. Alexis, 19, 32
*Joseph P. Kennedy, Jr.,* 152
Jupiter (missile), 35, 39, 72, 79, 110, 111, 163, 169–170

Kaiser, Philip M., 119, 120
Katzenbach, Nicholas de B., 9, 68, 73, 117

Keating, Sen. Kenneth, 2–3, 6, 29
Kennedy, President John F., 2, 5, 7, 11–12, 20n, 24, 26, 31–34, 36, 40, 44–45, 60–64, 69, 78, 104–106, 117, 147, 155, 169–174, 176–178, 183–188, 192–193
Kennedy, Robert, 8–9, 18, 32–33, 37n, 45, 51, 55, 60, 68, 121, 176, 178, 186–187
Kent, Sherman, 87
Khrushchev, Premier Nikita S., 2, 4, 8, 24, 27–28, 37–40, 125, 132–133, 148–149, 158–163, 166–167, 173, 180–182, 191
Knox, William, 132–136
Kohler, Foy, 37, 61
Komar torpedo boat, 14, 22
Kreisky, Bruno, 168
Kuznetsov, V. V., 182, 190

Lincoln, Mrs. Evelyn, 58
Linkins, Carroll, 76
Lippmann, Walter, 139–140
Loginov, V. A., 146
Lovett, Robert A., 64–65
Lyon, Cecil, 93, 127

McCloy, John J., 33, 97, 190
McCone, John A., 2, 7–9, 12, 13, 15, 19, 23, 28, 64, 166
Macmillan, Prime Minister Harold, 95, 111, 127–128, 146
McNamara, Robert S., 15, 18, 31–32, 38, 67, 77–78, 108, 135–137, 172, 180
McNaughton, John, 117
Mann, Thomas C., 49, 91
Manning, Robert, 85
Mariel (Cuban port), 6
Martin, Edwin M., 22, 32, 67, 79, 88, 107
*Marucla,* 152–153
May, Donald, 85
Meeker, Leonard C., 59, 73, 99
Mena, Ortiz, 91, 100
Merchant, Livingston, 82

MIG (plane), 14, 22, 55, 97, 123
Mikoyan, Anastas, 189
Minow, Newton, 101
Monroe Doctrine, 35, 51
Morgan, Edward P., 3
Murrow, Edward R., 55, 71

Nagy, Imre, 24
National Photographic Interpretation Center, 19
National Security Council, 33, 90, 99
Navarro, Emilio A., 8
Neubert, Joseph, 164
*Newport News*, 124
Nicholson, Sir Godfrey, 147
Nitze, Paul, 21–22, 39, 87n, 134, 170
Nixon, Richard M., 2

O'Brien, Lawrence F., 91
O'Donnell, Kenneth, 32, 43, 75, 170
*Omsk*, 29–30
Organization of American States (OAS), 112–114
Oribe, Emilio, 113
Ormsby Gore, Sir David, 53, 60, 70, 83, 89–90, 121

Pavicevic, Misa, 107
Penkovskiy, Col. Oleg, 24, 39
Philbriglex-62 (military exercise), 86
Phleger, Herman, 81
Pigott, Paul J., 19
Pigott, Theiline M., 7
Polonik, Mikhail, 116
*Poltava*, 29, 30, 116
Power, Gen. Thomas S., 98, 187
Powers, Francis Gary, 14–15, 49
Profumo, John, 128
PSALM (code name), 46

Quaison-Sackey, Alex, 115, 130

Reischauer, Edwin O., 126

Remedios, Cuba, 29, 75, 134
Reston, James, 25, 83
Reynolds, Lt. Cmdr. K. C., 153
Ribicoff, Abraham, 43
Rio Treaty, 35
Rivero, Vice Adm. Horacio, 123
Rockefeller, Gov. Nelson, 141
Roosevelt, Franklin D., 75, 139
Rusk, Dean, 14, 20, 26, 32, 33, 36, 40, 45, 55–57, 64, 82, 107–108, 110, 112–113, 134, 143, 157, 170, 184
Russell, (Bertrand) Earl, 126
Russell, Sen. Richard, 102

Sagua la Grande, Cuba, 75, 134
Salinger, Pierre, 69, 76, 85, 98, 129, 154, 171
SAM (surface-to-air missiles), 7–11, 13–15, 17, 100
San Cristóbal, Cuba, 15–17, 30–31, 46, 75, 134
Sarmiento Carruncho, Emilio, 113
Sarper, Selim, 170
Sato, Eifaku, 59
Scali, John, 3, 155–158
Schirra, Walter, 32
Schroeder, Gerhard, 20
Scott, Paul, 70
Senghor, President Leopold, 119
Siscoe, Joseph, 185
Smedberg, Vice Adm. William R., 123
Smith, Bromley, 171
Sonnenfeldt, Helmut, 164
Sorensen, Theodore, 32, 53, 74
Springsteen, George, 68
Stalin, Josef, 25
Stephansky, Ben, 113
Stephenson, Sir Hugh, 60, 70
Stevenson, Adlai, 32, 36, 45, 48, 79, 89, 107, 114, 130, 150–151, 154, 185
*Stickell*, 81
Strauss, Franz Joseph, 111
Strong, Maj. Gen. Sir Kenneth, 52–53, 60, 70
Sweeney, Gen. Walter C., 84

Sylvester, Arthur, 85–86, 133–134, 142

Talbot, Philips, 86
Taylor, Gen. Maxwell, 18, 32, 68, 186
Thompson, Llewellyn, 34–36, 40, 66, 72, 158 165, 168, 180, 191
Touré, President Sekou, 119
Truman, Harry S, 64

U Thant, 107, 115, 131–132, 148, 155, 175, 182, 185, 188
U-2 (plane), 10–11, 14–16, 36, 99, 172, 175, 178, 186

Van Zandt, Congressman James, 141
Voelkerfreund, 140

Ward, Vice Adm. Alfred G., 123
Ward, Dr. Stephen T., 127–129
White, Lincoln, 154
Whitney, John Hay, 92
Wiener, Ernest G., 116
Wilder, Cmdr. Tracy, 81
Wilson, Donald, 55, 71, 90, 100–101, 183
Wilson, Woodrow, 75, 139
Wohlstetter, Roberta, 23
Wright, Col. John R., 15, 17

Yarmolinsky, Adam, 117
Yevtushenko, Yevgeni, 144

Zablocki, Congressman Clement, 155
Zorin, Valerian, 48, 107, 115, 150–151, 182

## ABOUT THE AUTHOR

ELIE ABEL, a seasoned foreign correspondent, is known across the country for his special reports and analyses on NBC television. Before joining the National Broadcasting Company in 1961, he served ten years with *The New York Times* at home and overseas, covering the Defense and State Departments, summit conferences, the Hungarian revolution of 1956 and the Tibetan uprising of 1959. He also put in two years as Washington bureau chief of *The Detroit News*.

In 1965, he became chief of the NBC News bureau in London.